PRAISE FOR *THE WAY OF GRACE*

"As inspiring as it is practical, *The Way of Grace* is a lovely, inviting, and yes, gracious companion for walking the spiritual path."

GENEEN ROTH
author of the *New York Times* bestseller *Women Food and God* and *This Messy Magnificent Life*

"This book invites us to encounter the sheer grace that is the center of our own being through a willingness to fully digest our own experience, whatever it looks like. A practical and grounded guide to the spiritual wisdom at our core. A gem of a book."

ROGER HOUSDEN
author of the Ten Poems series, including *Ten Poems for Difficult Times*

"Miranda has given us a loving and lucid guide for the journey of spiritual surrender. For anyone ready to give up the struggle and relax into the arms of the Divine, this beautiful book will show you the way. This is a great gift to our world."

MARCI SHIMOFF
New York Times bestselling author of *Happy for No Reason*

"Miranda's luminous and precise insights melt old paradigms of awakening and spirituality that too often impede our actual blossoming. This book and its powerful practices for ego relaxation are a literal godsend for anyone who is tired of 'heroic' striving and thirsty for the nectar of Grace to bless every last corner of your life. Miranda illuminates the path home to our embodied Self with the tenderness of a beloved mother, the lyricism of a poet, and the rigorous, unyielding wisdom of a master."

STEPHEN DINAN, CEO
The Shift Network, author of *Sacred America, Sacred World*

"Miranda MacPherson offers a wise blessing, a mothering caress, and a sweet balm. You'll inhale the fragrance of grace. You'll notice yourself relaxing, understanding, forgiving, softening, allowing, and coming to rest. And having rested, may you discover yourself able to relax into beneficial action as never before."

TERRY PATTEN
author of *A New Republic of the Heart* and *Integral Life Practice*

"Miranda Macpherson is the hollow reed through which an enormously alive current of feminine wisdom flows. Let the thirsty cup of your heart be filled with this stream of practical, deliciously subversive, luminous nectar. Nondual awakening is not some detached and impersonal condition, but rather a warm and intimate state of being, generous and restful, drenched in grace."

MIRABAI STARR
author of *God of Love: A Guide to the Heart of Judaism, Christianity, and Islam* and *Caravan of No Despair: A Memoir of Loss and Transformation*

"*The Way of Grace* gives fresh perspective on letting go and allowing our true nature to shine forth. These teachings, relevant to our time, upgrade and update our understanding of Grace and give us the skillful and compassionate tools to facilitate ego giving way to freedom, joy, and liberation. This is a groundbreaking book."

LAMA PALDEN DROLMA
founder of Sukhasiddhi Foundation, author of *Love on Every Breath*

"*The Way of Grace* takes the reader on a journey of Self-discovery with Miranda Macpherson's gentle but masterful presence leading the way. Her soft, clear, and direct approach weaves practical meditation applications, inquiries, and examples that beckon the reader into direct experience of the Divine. Not only does it flesh out the depth and dimensions of Grace, at the same time it addresses our most important human concerns, showing us that grace is truly a way of being in this world from a consciousness beyond it."

DAVID HOFFMEISTER
author of *Unwind Your Mind Back to God: Experiencing A Course in Miracles*

"Grace is at the very heart of the spiritual journey, yet few of us know how to ride its currents. Miranda does. She has walked the subtle path of grace and carries its gifts. In these pages, she offers precise, step-by-step guidance for relaxing the grip of ego—one of the true secrets of authentic Self-realization. These teachings are powerful alchemy, and Miranda transmits them with beauty and Presence. *The Way of Grace* is eloquent, wise, and deeply helpful—a book to guide and inspire your ongoing awakening."

SALLY KEMPTON
author of *Meditation for the Love of It* and *Awakening Shakti*

"*The Way of Grace* is a luminous gift to our world. Miranda's wisdom, beauty, and depth shines through every page, carrying a living transmission of Grace, while artfully combining wisdom from decades of study, self-inquiry, and clinical application. This inspirational, uncommonly well-written book has the power to transform our individual and collective lives. Miranda Macpherson is one of the great teachers of our time."

SHAUNA SHAPIRO, PHD
professor, and author of *The Art and Science of Mindfulness* and *Mindful Discipline*

"Wherever our mind projects another as separate from ourselves, there is fear. And while the opposite of fear is love, love has no opposite. Herein lies the peace that passeth all understanding. Miranda speaks to the heart of this timeless truth in her book, *The Way of Grace*, where 'grace' is just another word for 'love.' She speaks eloquently that grace, like love, is always present. We just need to get out of its way so that love can truly blossom within ourselves and in our daily life, actions, and relationships. Reading her book is like going on retreat with Miranda and recovering what is always waiting patiently within ourselves: indestructible love and well-being as solid ground from which we can meet, face, overcome, and be transformed by every adversity and circumstance we'll ever face during our lifetime. Miranda languages the timeless truths of grace and love that we all can benefit from hearing, time and again, so that we can ever more fully lean into and bring forward in our lives and relationships."

RICHARD MILLER, PHD
author of *iRest Meditation: Restorative Practices for Health, Resiliency, and Well-Being*

"Grace is what one is always seeking. For no matter the activity or concern, it is only by a gift of grace that the ultimate luminous reality opens to us. The beautiful ambition of an awakened being is to awaken others. Miranda is such a being, and this precious book is an expression of her grace-bestowing nature."

RAZ INGRASCI
chairman and teacher, Hoffman Institute International

THE WAY OF GRACE

ALSO BY MIRANDA MACPHERSON

Meditations on Boundless Love: Teachings and Practices to Relax the Ego, Surrender Spiritual Resistance, and Rest in Your Vast Heart (Audio CD)

Boundless Love: Transforming Your Life with Grace and Inspiration

THE WAY OF GRACE

The Transforming Power of Ego Relaxation

Miranda Macpherson

SOUNDS TRUE
BOULDER, COLORADO

Sounds True
Boulder, CO 80306

Published 2018

All names and identifying details have been changed to protect the privacy of individuals.

Cover design by Jennifer Miles
Book design by Beth Skelley

Printed in Canada

Library of Congress Cataloging-in-Publication Data

Names: Macpherson, Miranda, author.
Title: The way of grace : the transforming power of ego relaxation / Miranda Macpherson.
Description: Boulder, Colorado : Sounds True, 2018. | Includes bibliographical references.
Identifiers: LCCN 2018008534 (print) | LCCN 2018023064 (ebook) |
ISBN 9781683641315 (ebook) | ISBN 9781683641308 (pbk.)
Subjects: LCSH: Spiritual life.
Classification: LCC BL624 (ebook) | LCC BL624 .M29323 2018 (print) | DDC 204—dc23
LC record available at https://lccn.loc.gov/2018008534

10 9 8 7 6 5 4 3 2 1

For God,
for my students,
and for you, dear reader

To Denise
wishing you deep rest,
peace and every
blessing in your life.
Love,
Miranda
www.mirandamacpherson.com

CONTENTS

FOREWORD

Grace. It is such a simple and beautiful word—a word that tends to lighten our mood and inspire us when we hear it. Regardless of our spiritual background, and even if we have not been much interested in spirituality as such, we can recognize something that has been here all along, in the background of our awareness, and arising more explicitly in our transitions and transformations. When we stop to consider it, we generally have some personal sense of being "touched by grace." Yet to what, exactly, does this word refer?

Grace is not "a thing." It is not something we can touch, although we may feel touched by it. It is not something we can see, although we may very well see *the effects* of Grace on ourselves and others. It is not something that we can hear, yet we may feel called by it. And it is not something we can taste, yet there is some particular sense to it, and some tastes may remind us of its presence.

Further, Grace is not an emotion, although it may produce many emotions—even profound states of feeling. It is not a thought, though when we have experienced it, we are likely to have a lot of thoughts about it! It is not a sensation, although the action of Grace may well produce many sensations in our body. We begin to realize that what we are seeking to understand is beyond the usual categories of objects and sensory experiences by which we usually navigate the world. To find the realm of Grace, we need to look deeper.

Clearly, as with all the most important inner elements of being a human being, Grace is something subtle, and found in the deepest places in our hearts, in the very fabric of our consciousness. Its presence is unmistakable—and we do indeed learn to recognize the sensory signals that let us know we are in the proximity of this mystery.

And even then, it takes a long time to really understand how to dance with this inner partner—how to surrender to its profound and astonishing influence.

In this book, Miranda Macpherson helps us come closer to understanding this mystery by breaking it down into four aspects or components. First, she shows us that Grace is a way of experiencing the ground of our humanity—the very foundation of our consciousness. In the traditions behind the Enneagram and the work that I do, we call this our *essence*. While it is interesting to talk about essence and to seek some way of defining it, it is best understood experientially, and Miranda guides us into inquiries, meditations, and practices that will do just that. We come to recognize a deeper layer of our Self that is here as background, regardless of whatever else we may be experiencing. Further, it is contact with these deeper dimensions of our experience that produce real and lasting change in us, as we will see.

Second, *The Way of Grace* shows us the tremendous blessings and benefit that come from contact with our essential nature. It is a huge relief when we discover the gentle and expansive qualities of our essential being. It holds our difficulties with patience, compassion, and loving kindness, and we learn to trust that this inner fountain of benevolence is always available. We merely forget its existence in the daily preoccupations of our ego and its agendas. Yet in a breath, a pause, a single moment when we are willing to notice and sense into the deeper layers of our being, this miraculous quality of blessing is always present, waiting for us.

Thirdly, Miranda helps us see that it is this blessing of Grace that actually transforms us, both psychologically and spiritually. To understand this, it is useful to think of our Self as being a dynamic relationship between our usual sense of self—what is commonly called our ego consciousness—and the deeper ground of essence of which we were just speaking. We learn that Grace is not a bypass of our egoic life and its attendant suffering; rather, Grace brings light and compassion to our pain and difficulties and actually transmutes them into something useable for our growth. Grace gives us the capacity to *be with* our experiences so that they can be digested and integrated into our soul's greater purpose. There is no "spiritual bypass" here. We are bringing loving awareness to our distress—*not* denying its existence. Grace gives us the grounded presence and lightness of heart that lets us stay, even with our historic pain and fear. It is this vital distinction that helps us live the truths we are learning and make them part of our lived lives.

Lastly, the transforming power of Grace helps us live our realization in the world—in our work and in our relationships. As Miranda mentions in this book, realizations can happen in a moment, but learning to integrate them in a way that supports our lived lives takes time and persistence. Many seekers get into trouble thinking that their realization experience marks the end of their journey, while many elements of their suffering remain unhealed. Grace teaches us to slow down, to enjoy the ongoing discoveries and flavors of our existence while growing in our sense of love and service in this world. It teaches us to meet our shame and fear and anger with consciousness and tenderness. We stop berating ourselves for our apparent lack of progress and get interested in what is arising in our consciousness moment by moment.

Really, Grace teaches us to live in two worlds at the same time, and ultimately, to see that they really are one. We learn to embody the essential qualities of our consciousness and discern the meaning of the spiritual advice "to be in the world but not of it." We find blessings in the small events of daily life—we "see God in a teacup," and realize that the power of Grace is always right here and right now. We recognize the preciousness of our journey, of our relationships, and of the people who are in our lives, and learn to appreciate every step of our journey as we take it. And we understand this is not a race with a finish line; we will be dancing with Grace and realizations of deeper aspects of ourselves for the rest of our lives. Participating in this ever-deepening and ever-expanding dance is our greatest joy.

If we take in this teaching deeply, we will come to recognize the centrality of learning to *surrender*. This may sound easy to some, but as we embark on the journey of surrender, we will likely realize that little in our lives has really taught us how to engage this dance. We eventually discover that we do not *decide* to surrender. If we still think of it as a decision that we can choose or not, we have not yet fully understood what surrender is. We come to see that surrender is not an action we can take—it is really found more in *seeing a greater truth*. When we open to the deeper dimensions of our experience while we are engaged in the day-to-day challenges of life, we start to see that we are not directing our lives in the way we may have imagined, and that greater forces are at work within us and around us.

Seeing this, something in our soul relaxes. Without exactly deciding to, we let go on a deeper level, and the transforming powers of Grace guide us through the experience to a new sense of ourselves and of life. As we will see in the pages of this book, so much of inner work is really a process of helping our frightened ego patterns to relax into the ground of being and discovering that doing so brings us everything we have been seeking.

We might well wonder what role we play in this process. Clearly, we are not in charge of our own transformation—the ego does not fix the ego—and at the same time, we know that passivity is not going to help us much either. What is required? As it turns out, our active attention attracts the action of Grace. We become *actively receptive*—consciously inviting the divine awareness in us and around us to do what needs doing. This orientation toward our experience takes some practice, and thankfully, Miranda provides supports, practices, and relevant examples throughout the book to help us find the living balance of active attention and receptivity—no small feat and an incredibly important teaching for any serious seeker.

This important book is a feast of wisdom tradition, practice, and spiritual poetry, blended together by the steady and compassionate voice of Miranda Macpherson. We can feel the experience and wisdom here, distilled from years of practice as well as from seeing what works and what does not.

In so many ways, Miranda is an exquisite guide for this journey, taking us by the hand and embodying all the principles she is describing. We can actually feel this as we read the text, as if there is a dear friend at our side. Her words weave a field of holding that allows us to take a chance, and to step outside the familiar realms of our ego patterns. Step by step we come to understand what she means by ego relaxation. She kindly invites us to drop into the mystery of our own depth, while being sensitively aware of the fears and reactions that inevitably arise as we do. Her wisdom helps us address those fears and issues every step of the way.

You will also notice that Miranda is conversant in a wide range of spiritual traditions and shows how the different aspects of Grace are held in these diverse perspectives. We cannot help but notice the respect with which she holds each of these traditions, inviting us into the exploration from wherever we may have begun our journey. She moves seamlessly between the great traditions of the East and West, and between psychology and spirituality. In doing so, she helps us recognize the organic nature of our undertaking while also having a fresh appreciation of the aspiration of these traditional teachings.

What will be most encouraging for many of us is her willingness to share her own journey, and she lets us into her moments of vulnerability, confusion, and difficulty, helping us see how her being with those experiences opened doors to the breakthroughs of Grace that transformed her life. Again and again, we will see how the principles of Grace and the barriers to its unfolding are dealt with in real human ways.

Beyond the gems of wisdom throughout the book, Miranda also provides an array of real tools that can be used for the rest of your life. There are exercises, prayers, and meditations after each lesson providing opportunities to inquire into our own direct experience of the topics. She lays them out, one by one, taking us through the barriers to Grace as we move deeper and deeper into the mystery. If you actually engage the practices—and I hope you do—you will discover that while the lessons must be put into some kind of order so we can learn them, they also *accumulate*. As you progress in the book, you will find that the lessons are coalescing into a new sense of you, and this indeed is the work of Grace.

What is truly special about this book is that it so successfully combines theory and practice in a way that is certain to produce real transformation in any students seriously taking on its exercises and lessons. As a teacher of the Enneagram, I am often asked by students who have discovered something about their core ego patterns and discerned the deeper dimensions of their souls, "What can I do? Can you suggest a resource that will help me continue my work with this material?"

It is rare to find the relevant practical teachings gathered in one place, but you will find them here. I can wholeheartedly recommend the work contained in *The Way of Grace* as a magnificent foundation for the inner work needed to make use of maps of consciousness such as the Enneagram or Core Dynamics. So by all means, dig in, and may you find what your heart is seeking.

RUSS HUDSON
New York City
May 12, 2018

INTRODUCTION

Grace is always present. You imagine it is something somewhere
high in the sky, far away, and has to descend. It is really inside you,
in your Heart, and the moment you merge the mind into its Source,
Grace rushes forth, sprouting as from a spring from within you.

RAMANA MAHARSHI, ***The Essential Teachings of Ramana Maharshi***
(by Matthew Greenblatt)

Perhaps you hunger to finally end the struggle of living from the consciousness of fear and separation. Perhaps you yearn for a saner, wiser, more spiritually elegant way to move through our world that is so painfully lacking in Grace. You might have tasted luminous moments of freedom. Yet often the distance between what you have glimpsed and how you actually live can seem like an unbridgeable chasm. Perhaps you are weary of the dizzying pace of a culture that drives us ever further from our true nature. If you are disillusioned by the spiritual struggle to triumph over your ego, I have good news for you. There is another way: a way of Grace. This book is a hand of spiritual friendship to help you close the gap and come to abide in the living presence that you are and always were. At home within, you can find a radiant new way of being, extending love, clarity, and peace deeper into our troubled world.

It is usually when you are not trying so hard that Grace emerges. Just before my thirty-sixth birthday, I traveled to Arunachala, a sacred mountain in South India that was home to the revered sage Sri Ramana Maharshi. One impossibly hot and airless day, I sat down on a threadbare cushion in a dark musty cave and settled into meditation. For once, I was not trying to get anywhere. A thunderous silence emerged, reverberating with this transmission:

Be nothing.
Do nothing.
Get nothing.
Become nothing.
Seek for nothing.
Relinquish nothing.
Be as you are.
Rest in God.

It was complete stillness—alive with an unshakable presence. Prior to this, I was intimate with the Divine as a scintillating ocean of light, boundless love. But this was an entirely new dimension of Grace. Like merging into the velvety blackness of the infinite night sky, it was beyond any concept or definition I had ever known. Any sense of "I," other, world, and even God disappeared. All commentary dropped, all thought stopped, all effort disappeared. No-thing-ness—not a deficient story but liberated pure beingness—was shining, and I was that.

I remained in this state for approximately three weeks. Everything was the same and yet totally different. It was profoundly easeful and direct. There was no need to fix anything. No need to get anything. No need for anything to happen or not happen. Nothing I had to do. Even a growing pile of rubbish on the street was fine. The impetus to control and manipulate the universe to fit some ideal had disappeared. I had landed in the sweet state that I now call "ego relaxation." I felt utterly natural, settled in the primordial condition, and part of the mystery that animates this world. It took me years to fully understand the significance of this transmission, let alone fully digest it. Over time, it birthed a map for a holistic approach to nondual realization and a potent body of teachings and practices that I am so happy to share with you in this book.

TRANSMISSION OF GRACE

Grace has a way of stopping you in your tracks. It often comes with a transmission, an energetic communication from a higher state than our linear mind can understand. Grace always requires some kind of surrender, what Indian traditions call "dropping the mind into the heart." This can feel unnerving, or even downright insulting to our familiar way of navigating through life. When I shared this transmission in London for the first time, a red-haired woman with a thick, cockney accent protested, saying: "Be nothing, do nothing, get nothing, become nothing: What good can that do me? I do not want to live a dull, colorless, boring life."

Our ego presumes that surrender will be the end of the color, the juice, and the fun. Paradoxically, the opposite is true. The more I learned to rest in the open, empty spaces, the more Grace came alive inside—literally, as Ramana says, "sprouting as a spring from within." It can for you too.

WHAT *IS* GRACE?

Grace is way more than a beautiful state that fills your heart with gratitude. Rumi described it when he said, "Something opens our wings. Something makes boredom and hurt disappear. Someone fills the cup in front of us."[1] Grace is the living presence that brings online the qualities of your true nature, such as love, peace, joy, strength, clarity, inherent intelligence, and so much more. These divine qualities are sewn into the very fabric of your being, so they are always present. However, they are covered by many adaptive layers that must be addressed if you are to gain access. Grace brings forth precisely what you need to heal, evolve, and thrive so that your noble qualities can flow deeper into our world. Grace also brings blessings from celestial realms, whether or not you have "faith" in anything particular.

Grace has four primary dimensions, or ways that it comes alive. These dimensions form the structure of this book. Briefly, Grace is simultaneously the unchanging *ground* of your being; the *blessings* that refine, uplift, and nourish you; the *transforming power* that lifts your veils; and ultimately, a more easeful, spiritually elegant *way of being in this world* from a consciousness way beyond it. But every dimension of Grace needs space. It needs you to empty out your fixed positions and presumptions, sometimes even your cherished spiritual ones. Would you be willing to hold on to nothing?

WHATEVER YOU LEAVE EMPTY, GRACE CAN FILL

The transmission that emerged in Ramana's cave was the beginning of a quantum shift in identity. The two years that followed were a powerful period of undoing all that prevented its embodiment. It was the deep spiritual winter of my life, where I was pruned back to the root. Like learning to appreciate the starker landscape of winter, the more I emptied out, the more it revealed its own kind of beauty. Many structures of my familiar identity started falling away. This included a marriage of thirteen years, my role as the spiritual director of a groundbreaking interfaith seminary in London, the city I called home, and all but a few friends. Even practices that had been my well of spiritual nourishment for years no longer fed me. It felt as though a giant hand was sweeping over the chessboard of my life, knocking all the pieces to the floor. I was standing on the edge of the void, being invited to voluntarily drop in completely, with no idea of what might be on the other side.

Sometimes we are brought to a pivotal crossroads in life. You might even be at one right now. Navigating change gracefully all hinges on your capacity to say *yes* to what's happening, rather than *no*. Thankfully, twenty years of prior spiritual practice had developed my inner musculature enough to say yes. This period of fierce Grace was not easy, but ultimately it was very helpful. Miraculously, the strength and guidance as to what to say and do emerged, even though I had to adapt to a level of vulnerability that felt like having no outer skin. The more I surrendered in and through what was, the more I came alive like never before. I felt so vividly in touch with the primordial pulse that birthed us all into being. Best of all was a new fearlessness.

REALIZATION HAPPENS IN AN INSTANT; INTEGRATION TAKES TIME

Too often, spiritual awakening is presented as some gigantic spiritual orgasm, after which you are "done" with the muck and mess of being human. I will not do you such a disservice. Awakening can happen in a split second, but integrating its wisdom is a lengthier, nuanced process. It requires ongoing practice even though you are not aiming to fix yourself. Spiritual openings inevitably dislodge hidden corners of our psyche we did not know existed; therefore, authentic embodiment demands psychological unpacking and usually the support of an elder on the path. You might hear some teachers say that including the psychological keeps you in your "story," but I have seen more seekers getting stuck in their story by refusing to face what needs to be faced.

A HOLISTIC, FEMININE APPROACH TO AWAKENING

Just as nature does not reject anything but integrates and includes all that has come before in her evolution, so we must learn to include all that arises as we walk the way of Grace. The practice of ego relaxation, which we will be working with throughout this book, not only makes you receptive to all dimensions of Grace, but also powerfully heals the parts of the ego that cannot let go without sufficient love. This is especially the case for westerners, whose ego has formed amidst greater cultural complexity compared to thousands of years ago, when ancient traditions were unfolding.

There were times, especially in that first year after receiving the transmission, when I was just like any other woman going through the difficulties of divorce, losing everything familiar, and at times feeling like a raw traumatized animal shivering on the floor. All of the models of spiritual realization I had worked with previously, which had been delivered through the masculine lens only, might have viewed my process as a failure to remain in the no-self state. However, the transmission of ego relaxation revealed a much more integrated, feminine approach to walking the path—to surrender *in and through* all that we encounter, including our animal humanity and all of our emotions. When I say "feminine" I do not mean that this is just for those with a vagina. The way of Grace is for humanity. Its objective is to love everyone back into the full embodiment of who we really are. This is a lot more effective than beating yourself into spiritual shape, which is not the compassionate response our world needs.

A COSMIC DANCE OF EMPTINESS AND FULLNESS

As an interfaith minister, I had always revered the great wisdom traditions as distinct streams but ultimately not separate from the one ocean of Truth. I have loved studying their scriptures and engaging many of their practices. I even spent a decade ushering mature seekers through a powerful curriculum based on the spiritual technologies each tradition offers to liberate our true nature.

If you have explored some of the Eastern traditions of Buddhism, Vedanta, and Taoism, you will have noticed that true nature is emphasized as emptiness, spaciousness, and witnessing awareness. Thus their practices focus on dissolving the self, emptying into the void of pure mystery, and abiding in spaciousness. If you have studied the Western traditions, perhaps mystical Christianity, Kabbalah, or Sufism, you will have noticed quite a different emphasis on the relationship between God and the human soul and that their practices focus on cultivating the virtues that refine and elevate our consciousness. I am not sure we can ever separate a tradition from the culture from which it arose. Eastern cultures in general are way more collectivist, and Western cultures cherish the individual.

I come out of a Christian culture and have always been devotional by nature, with a Sufi heart and a Hindu soul . . . for reasons I cannot explain other than reincarnation. Embracing "no-thing and no-one" led to the integration of all that I had studied for so many years. No-thingness (emptiness) and living presence (full of every divine attribute) began to feel like a cosmic union at my core and the core of all things. This divine lovemaking is constantly taking place in the paradoxes we regard as heaven and earth, body and spirit, form and formlessness. This synthesis came alive within through an inner teacher that had no face or name. That same inner teacher lives inside you too.

ALREADY WITHIN THE LIVING WATER

Even if you have years of sincere spiritual study and practice under your belt, it is easy to get caught up in what I call the "thirsty fish syndrome," seeking the living water that can truly quench your thirst, while not recognizing that you are already in and part of it. You might have heard of the term *nonduality*, which literally means "not two." Nondual awakening is important because it dissolves separation, ending the search for love, peace, and freedom. It restores awareness that you are and have always been in and part of everything you always wanted. Nondual awakening means not only tasting Grace but also recognizing that you *are* Grace. Yet you can't talk yourself into this. You cannot intellectualize or theorize. You must enter more deeply into your own direct experience and surrender. Then the mystery that has been living through you all this time has space to come freshly alive.

Wherever you find yourself right now on the path, the transmission that reverberates through this whole book says: Be as you are. Rest in God. Right here, right now—with this. There is nowhere else you need to go. Not even to a cave in India. The Grace that came alive in that cave, and the transforming wisdom that emerged in the years since, has come to you.

May this book make that walk across the shore in your consciousness easier, kinder, and more potent. May it bring infinite richness and meaning to your life and deeper peace to our troubled world. May Grace become our *way*.

About the Practices

Each of the following chapters contains powerful practices to facilitate you into direct experience. There are reflections, inquiries, and meditation practices. With the inquiry questions, I recommend reflecting or journaling into them, letting your response be detailed and unedited. Better still would be to invite a friend to offer these questions to you for at least ten minutes, with no commentary—only the question, a little space, and a thank you for whatever you share. Then switch roles. It is *crucial* that your partner does not offer solutions to address your "issues." That will pull you out of inquiry into ego fixing!

Holistic self-inquiry is not thinking, but journeying. Let the questions enter into your *body*, noticing the sensations and energy that arise; your *heart*, noticing the feelings; and your *mind*, letting the insights come. The more detailed and dimensional you are as you work with these questions, the more they will open you.

PART I

RELAXING INTO THE GROUND OF GRACE

When you are not, the whole of existence comes into you.
When the drop disappears, it becomes the ocean.

OSHO, ***Tantra: The Supreme Understanding***

There is way more support to help you surrender beyond your struggle into a life of authentic beauty and meaning than you can imagine. Let me introduce you to what I call the ground of Grace. The primary reason most people struggle to gain real traction on the path, even after years of dedication, is that it has not occurred to them that there could be some true ground to relax into.

When you identify with your personality as who you are, it feels as if you have to somehow create the support and strategize to keep safe. You believe that you are the one who has to make it happen. These presumptions feel so normal that you might not even stop to question them. Your body braces, your breath becomes shallow, your heart pulls back, and then your mind gets busy thinking and commentating. It is all a reaction from a felt sense of disconnection from Grace as your natural foundation. Until you recognize what you are always in and supported by, the mind just cannot quiet down, let alone surrender.

Yet consider this: Each day the sun rises and sets, and seeds turn into all kinds of plants that produce shelter, beauty, food, and oxygen to sustain your life. Something causes your heart to beat and is causing you to draw breath right now. Notice how this all happens without the need for any effort on your part.

Consider how you emerged into this world, how anyone came to be here, and what makes you interested in reading this book. Something primordial and beneficent is pulsing through us all. You cannot see it with your physical eyes, yet the evidence is everywhere, animating all things. This is the underlying ground of Grace. It is the cause of your being and all being. This is what you can let all of your concerns and fears relax down into. Your ego defenses and all of your complicated history can melt into a mountainous presence that gives you true support to be as you truly are.

Turning more substantially within, you will inevitably meet the dense forces of ego fear, control, and judgment that everyone meets on the way home. It does not serve to deny or bypass them, for even after significant openings, these defenses can easily reemerge. The next four chapters provide a map to gracefully allow true surrender, opening beyond fear, control, and judgment. First, let me introduce you to the practice of ego relaxation, which makes this all possible.

1 SURRENDER

The Practice of Ego Relaxation

Just sit there right now.
Don't do a thing.
Just rest.

For your separation from God
Is the hardest work in this world.

Let me bring you trays of food
And something
That you like to drink.

You can use my soft words
As a cushion
For your
Head.

HAFIZ, *The Subject Tonight Is Love*
(translated by Daniel Ladinsky)

Surrender is the heart of all spiritual paths. It is what brings all four dimensions of Grace alive. Yet our culture equates surrender with defeat, losing, giving up to another ego will: "Okay, I surrender! You win!" Perhaps you are willing to surrender, sincerely desiring transformation from entrenched ego patterns and reactions. Yet surrender is often misunderstood as trying to amputate the frustrating habits of your personality that you think should not be there.

Surrender is the great conundrum of the spiritual path because the self who is trying to surrender is the one blocking the way. How then can we authentically yield into the ground of Grace?

EGO RELAXATION, NOT EGO ANNIHILATION

To live into the promises of awakening, we must somehow turn the hard chunk of ice that is our ego fixation back into the fluid state of its origin. Up until very recently, most spiritual teachings, in both the East and the West, have been given from a masculine perspective. This has often lent itself to a macho approach of hacking away at our ego tendencies, like taking an axe to the ice. While this might break the ego down, it is hard work and can easily turn into aggression toward our humanity in the name of awakening. Ego annihilation engenders fear, creates unnecessary resistance, and can even build a more spiritualized ego, strengthening the delusion you are in charge of the show. While dedication, rigor, and discipline are important, so too are compassion, mercy, kindness, and, most of all, love.

Consider how the fundamental substance of ice is still water, even though it may be hard, opaque, and dense. So too at the deepest level is your ego still part of the divine fabric of God—just frozen in fixed patterns and ignorant of its holiness. Understanding this nondual principle helps you recognize there is no enemy and thus nothing that needs to be hacked away. Rumi explained it when he said, "Be melting snow. Wash yourself of yourself."[1] True surrender is really a process of melting, yielding back into our primordial condition.

Just as the warmth of the sun will naturally transform the hard block of ice back to its original fluid state of water, exposing your dense, fixated patterns to the presence of loving awareness will melt the distortions. You don't do the melting; Grace does that. Your part is learning to just be here, right where you are, relaxing the usual attempts to do something, get somewhere, become different, seek for something other, and relinquish what you believe should not be there. Your job is to be present and undefended, facing everything, while ceasing and desisting your efforts to rearrange yourself. This is the practice of ego relaxation.

EGO RELAXATION IS BOTH A *TRANSMISSION* AND A *PRACTICE*

The transmission of ego relaxation provides a much-needed vacation from your story, silencing that bad radio station in your mind. Like a Zen koan, "Be nothing, do nothing, get nothing, become nothing, seek for nothing, relinquish nothing. Be as you are. Rest in God," interrupts your frantic ego grasping and rejecting. It invites your separate self, which has forgotten that it is being lived and moved by the Grace of the universe, to submit to the true master: the vast heart. Yet ego relaxation is not just a beautiful state of Grace, it is also a potent practice of ongoing surrender.

Ego relaxation asks for your commitment to being present while meeting your direct experience fully, without trying to make it different. You might feel relieved to hear that Grace does not ask you to fix yourself or amputate anything. It does not ask you to fulfill some ideal of perfection; it just asks you to be here and relax your defenses. Perhaps you feel relieved: "Thank God. I am so exhausted by all that hard work." Or perhaps you feel disbelief: "How could this possibly help me get past my bad habits?" Often, we do not trust that transformation can happen without punitive treatment and a ton of effort. Could surrender really be this simple?

BE PRESENT AND OPEN TO EVERYTHING

Ego relaxation is indeed very simple because it is ultimately not something you do; it is something that you allow. However, it takes discipline to drop out of your mind and be present, letting your defenses relax. It also requires courage, for it will mean allowing vulnerable feelings and then doing nothing to cover them over, change, or fix them. This is how you get out of the way. Once you learn that you will not die from feeling hurt, fear, anger, disappointment, or any manner of things, you become more surrendered. You discover that what actually surrenders is not technically you. Rather, it is your self-image, who you have taken yourself to be, that gives way. Then you naturally forgive your ego, yet without pandering to it. This means that the deeper truth in you "wins." Your wisdom can pour forth in ways that help and heal.

BE HERE AND BE STILL

Ego relaxation is easier when you are in a good mood or on the meditation cushion. It is more challenging to stay present when allowing difficult emotions like hurt, sadness, and anger, or while watching the news. Ego relaxation shows us how we can "be still" even in the face of intensity, within or without. Yet you cannot force stillness. Just as progressive muscle relaxation guides you to release physical tension by bringing awareness to a particular body part and then seeing if it can let go, the practice of ego relaxation brings loving awareness to the specifics of your direct experience, be it body tension, fearful constructs, difficult emotions, or circumstances. Instead of thinking about your experience, you contact it, without any manipulation. You just see what can melt. Just as you cannot force muscle tension to release, you cannot wage war on the material you find challenging. Ego relaxation welcomes you into what is, with patience and compassion. It transforms you by opening up inner space from the construct of self that usually predominates. As I am sure you know, this self is inherently limited, distorted, and full of stress.

This inner spaciousness makes you receptive to Grace, allowing it to come freshly alive, bringing forward what you most need. Ego relaxation offers unconditionally allowing arms to all parts of your being to just come home to the primordial condition. This is the ground in which everything can unwind and integrate.

EGO RELAXATION IS NOT PASSIVE OR RESIGNED

Ego relaxation is not mere navel gazing or checking out from full participation in life, relationships, and the world. It is a direct but kind invitation for the tense, historical, contracted "self" to resign as the director of your process. It is an invitation to settle and relax your resistance. It does not mean you collapse and do not pay your bills, or withdraw from tackling an important task or having that challenging conversation with your spouse. It is not to be misused as an excuse to avoid fulfilling your duties or behaving without integrity.

Genuine ego relaxation will make you less egocentric, more real, and more capable of walking the path substantially, facing whatever arises within you and within life from a place of spiritual maturity. It does this by relaxing the cause of your stress, conflict, and tension. A new possibility emerges for ease, synchronicity, and flow beyond your wildest imaginings. You become more potent and effective in ordinary life.

BEYOND TRYING, INTO GRACEFUL SURRENDER

The greatest challenge to Grace is the tendency to reconstellate around the notion that "I have to do it." The part of you that feels this inner pressure—including the pressure to understand ego relaxation—*is the one who is asked to relax*. We will unpack this more thoroughly in chapter 3, "Melting the Grip of Control." For now, remember that the way of Grace is not about making your ego enlightened. Rather, it is relaxing out of your ego construct as an ongoing process. You cannot force it, but you can engage the practice. You can learn to yield to a power deeper than your mind. The more you give up to Grace, the more you feel the loving support moving you to further surrender. Rumi describes it this way: "The ocean takes care of each wave until it reaches the shore."[2] Somehow, fear falls away, and Grace has its way with you.

You might ask, "If awakening ultimately happens by Grace anyway, what is my participatory role?" Essentially, you only ever have two choices: to let go or not to let go. The former opens you exponentially to a life of beauty and possibility; the latter just makes you suffer. It usually makes everyone around you suffer also. Yet even this question arises from the perspective of the ego. The more you practice ego relaxation, the more surrender just starts to take place. You naturally become more open and less defensive; your crunchy habits become less dense, or at the very least, you don't take your personality so seriously.

When true surrender actually happens, it feels very graceful. Like "you" are not "doing" anything. Ultimately, nobody really surrenders because there is no one to surrender. Surrender is really a bridge that helps make the transition from identifying as a separate someone to remembering you are in and part of the infinite ocean. The more you engage the practice of ego relaxation, the more you will see that there is something luminous inside, underneath your familiar "me," and it knows the way. Grace emerges, bringing the wisdom you need for precisely what life is serving up right now.

I do not ask you to take my word for it. When Jesus was asked by his disciples, "Where do you abide, Master?" he did not answer with a geographic location as we might if asked where we live. He responded with an invitation to "come and see." The following meditation can help you begin to experience the transmission of ego relaxation. This is the foundation for many of the other meditations we will engage in on this journey. Embrace it as a daily practice, as an entry into peaceful abiding. Take that true vacation from unnecessary stress and struggle often!

MEDITATION **Melting into Ego Relaxation**

1. Sit somewhere quiet and comfortable where you will not be disturbed.

2. Turn your focus inward, to the natural rise and fall of your breath.

3. Consider each inhale a "welcome."

4. Receive the molecules of the oxygen themselves as an unconditional gift from all plant life. Feel it welcoming you unconditionally to just be here however you are in this moment.

5. Consider each exhale an invitation to let something melt.

6. Without forcing anything away, see what can melt. Perhaps subtle tension in the muscles of your eyes, shoulders, neck, or belly. Perhaps the conversations you have had today can melt into the past. Perhaps the tasks, the shopping list, and the unread emails can melt away.

7. In this moment, what if you could just "be nothing, do nothing, get nothing, become nothing, seek for nothing, relinquish nothing"?

8. What's it like if you just be here, as you are? What if right now, you are already resting in God? Let go into the ocean of infinite Grace. Just rest. Just be.

9. If the grip of "I have to" arises, see who this "I" is. Greet it unconditionally, with the welcoming in-breath and the melting out-breath. No need to reject anything that arises.

10. Yet see what else is here.

11. See what can melt naturally with the compassionate allowing of your own breath. ~

Now let us further explore the practice of ego relaxation via three inquiry questions that guide you there.

INQUIRY **Ego Relaxation Practice**

Use this line of inquiry anytime you notice you are no longer present but caught in some struggle.

What limits you from dropping deeper and letting yourself be?
See what resistance arrives toward ego relaxation. Do not worry about where you *should* be but instead just see what actually limits you, without judgment. Whatever you find, remember you do not have to *do* anything about it. Just let it be met with unconditional allowing just as the sun warms whatever it contacts. Follow the thread of whatever you saw with the next question.

What does this provide that you think you need?
Any defense or resistance is held together by a presumption, fear, concern, or belief, whether conscious or unconscious. Again, see what wants to be brought to the light of unconditional awareness. Again, there's nothing to do. Just meet it.

Dig deep with the two questions above for at least ten minutes. Then take another ten minutes to journey further with the next question.

What's it like, in body, heart, and mind if you allow your direct experience to be exactly as it is?
Having met your resistance in the prior questions, with this question, you are invited to explore how the practice of ego relaxation affects you. Surf your inner terrain with as much detail as possible. Notice what happens when you are present, without resistance or commentary. ~

Ego relaxation is so simple, and yet it is a very advanced spiritual practice of nondoing. This is what can make it hard to grasp conceptually. Yet nothing I have found in three decades of guiding others in transformation is as powerful at bringing us into direct experience of the sacred. Ego relaxation settles your frantic ego. You become more accepting and more peaceful. The more you learn to just be here, not in your thoughts *about* your experience but directly dropped *into your direct experience*, the more you land deeper in Grace. Now you have a practice that can carry you through life's peaks and valleys, all the way home.

2 THERE IS NOTHING TO FEAR

I have no cause for anger or fear, for You surround me.
And in every need that I perceive, Grace suffices.

***A Course in Miracles Workbook*, Lesson 348**

Surrendering into the ground of Grace sounds heavenly. Yet until you discover how to open through the force of fear, you are bounced back into resistance, unable to let go into deeper states of Grace. Even after luminous moments, you can find yourself worshiping at the altar of familiar patterns, even when you know they cause you to suffer. What does it take to move beyond fear? Ego relaxation invites you *toward* your fear, to understand what it feeds on and to see who it protects. Surprisingly, when you open through your fear, not only does it dissolve but the energy within it can propel you into a whole other galaxy of freedom.

In my early twenties, I was digging deep with the teachings of *A Course in Miracles*, a metaphysical psycho-spiritual text that offers precise spiritual exercises for each day of the year. Its stated purpose is to unwind the consciousness of fear and reestablish God-consciousness. Forty-eight days into this journey, I landed on the lesson titled "There Is Nothing to Fear." While many of the daily lessons were complex, sprawling several pages to explain the practice and its logic, this lesson was three short, pragmatic paragraphs. It was so dystonic to my emotional reality at the time that I reverted to the previous forty-seven lessons, convinced that I must have missed something crucial.

At that time, I was fueled by so many everyday fears. Ploughing the contents of my mind, I found fear of abandonment, fear of failure, fear of weakness, fear of humiliation, fear of rejection, fear of intimacy, fear of being overwhelmed, fear of not getting what I wanted, fear of putting on weight, fear of aging, fear of death, and fear of the unknown. On top of that was the fear in the knowledge that all of these fears were sure to manifest! Even though my personality was not overtly anxious compared to many, in the earlier stages of the path, my mind was like a runaway train, recycling the past into the future. Even if you have an established practice that provides some spacious inner respite, it is not always easy to get off that runaway train and stop believing your fearful mind.

UNDERSTAND THE FORCE OF FEAR

Fear itself is not wrong. In its purity, it is a brilliant force of our survival instinct that will activate our body and mind into a state of high alert so we can respond in a split second to get out of harm's way—whether that be to slam our foot on the brakes to avoid a head-on collision, sprint to catch our child from falling into a swimming pool, or remove ourselves from emotional violence.

To walk the way of Grace, you must learn to discriminate between an authentic threat to your well-being and a *perceived* threat that contracts your mind into a consciousness of fear, distorting your perception of reality and blocking entry into refined states of Grace. Commonly, we are caught up in fearful patterns of mind, without even being fully aware of it.

ADDRESS THE FEAR OF GOING WITHIN

Who doesn't want entry into the bliss, beauty, and freedom that awakening promises? Yet gaining traction on the path invites the repressed feelings, forces, and impulses of your unconscious mind to be flushed up to the surface. This spiritual detoxification process is ultimately liberating, but it is not for sissies. The most common reason I hear for holding back from genuinely dropping deeper is fear of being overwhelmed by a Pandora's box of memories and feelings that we might not be able to stuff back down. This holds most people back from looking within much at all.

Remembering that we all exist within a ground of Grace provides the inner strength not to be scared off by the gargoyle at the gate to the sanctuary. Although the world is always changing and is by its nature uncertain, there is a deeper pulse underneath everything that causes the sun to rise and set each day, plants to compassionately absorb your carbon dioxide and give back life-giving oxygen, and Mother Earth to graciously welcome you, providing a home, food, and incredible beauty. This mysterious, ever-present ground of Grace is here even when your beloved companion is dying, you have lost your job, or you have been derailed by the unexpected.

YOU ARE ALREADY IN THE GROUND OF GRACE

I am not asking you to imagine this or take my word for it. Just bring your awareness into your feet and feel the ground underneath you right now. Receive the life-giving oxygen arriving naturally with each breath you automatically know how to take. Somehow, you exist within something much greater than your mind. This is also what caused you to emerge out of your mother's womb into this world, what causes your heart to beat, and what causes you to want to read the next line on this page. When you turn your awareness to recognize the immense power and love that is the unchanging ground of all being, you discover that there is more immediate support for you to just be here, where you are. This provides the strength you need to face your fear.

I once received an email from a brave woman who admitted, "I am terrified of the depth of myself." Our ego presumes there is something lurking in the basement of our being that is irreparably flawed, ugly, unacceptable, and defective. Everyone I have sat with across culture, gender, and age admits to hidden fears of feeling deficient in some way, even though they might never show this in any obvious way to the world. This is the primary reason most of us resist diving more substantially within—we are afraid that our carefully preserved self-image might crack. Yet spiritually, this is exactly what needs to happen. It is how we discover that we are far deeper, wiser, and more loving than we dreamed. Ultimately, true bravery is not being afraid of yourself.

FEAR ARISES FROM SEPARATION

Fearful patterns of mind are part of the human condition. They originate from feeling separate from our true nature, which is total love, peace, power, strength, and joy. The degree to which we identify with being a separate someone determines the intensity of our fear. Separation might sound abstract, but it is no joke. When we experience "I'm separate . . . ," whether we feel that as separation from God; from our mother, who seems to be the source of everything at first; from nature; from one another; or from love, strength, peace, or support, our body contracts and our heart shrinks. Then our mind gets busy, spinning strategies of defense that cost us contact with the peaceful present. We presume we must have done something wrong to be in this condition. A vague sense of shame descends, but for what exactly, we are not quite sure.

Our personality develops around our childhood experiences of separation and the work-arounds we discovered to make that more manageable. Over time, this becomes the primary track of our personality. Layer by layer, the mud of conditioning covers the luminous jewel of our being. We end up living on the surface of ourselves, ignorant of our vast and beautiful depths. We polish up the outer surface of the mud, not realizing that we are just living out of a self-image that is really just a shell. It will inevitably get cracked by the turning of life's wheel—whether that be from illness, loss of a cherished love affair, a dent to our pride, or ultimately the aging process, which demands we get with the program of graceful surrender.

PRACTICE EGO RELAXATION IN AND THROUGH YOUR FEAR

To simply affirm "there is nothing to fear" does not tackle the issue. That is like telling a child frightened of monsters under the bed to stop being afraid when the lights are turned out. No amount of reassurance resolves fear. Just as a child needs loving support to look directly into the lurking monster's abode to see whether or not it really exists, you must address fear directly and explore the disconnection that it emerges from. Ultimately, inquire, "Who it is that is so afraid?"

It is not enough to get this intellectually, by trying to rationalize your fear away. Liberating Grace emerges when you *meet* the layers of feeling, memory, belief, assumption, and projection and practice ego relaxation—just being here, doing nothing, and contacting whatever you find with unconditional love.

Whenever you meet fear honestly and directly, not as a story but as pure phenomenon, you begin to see deeper into the foundations of the fear. This usually births compassion and insight to support the next level of your liberation. Often, the fear itself simply dissolves.

If you do not penetrate into and through your fear, you can too easily live daily life *trying* not to feel deficient, *trying* to prove you are lovable, valuable, or good enough. This trying is the single greatest block to the experience of Grace. It turns your life into an endless self-improvement project centered in denial of a simple human fact: your ego actually *is* limited. All egos are fundamentally insecure because their nucleus is hollow, based in a sense of separation.

When you recognize that this is not something to be afraid of, you will discover that what you thought was a big problem is the gate to a game-changing realization: *You* are more than this. *You* are the one who is looking at the layers of fear. *You* are the loving awareness that is contacting memories, feelings, beliefs, assumptions, projections, and layers of conditioning. As Saint Francis of Assisi is reported to have said, "The one you are looking for is the one who is looking."

Inquiring into your fear then leads you into a fresh exploration of the basement of your being. You can discover that your foundation is not something ugly and deficient but Grace itself: infinite space, love without limit, joy without reason, and peace that surpasses all understanding. This Grace, which belongs to all of us, is not affected by our history and our personality, our mistakes and troubles, and it does not come or go. *This is why there is nothing to fear.*

One warm spring day I was sitting with James, an advanced meditator who asked for my support to work through the terror that was arising as his inner experience was expanding to a new level. I asked him, "How do you avoid dropping fully into your practice?"

He shared all kinds of distracting habits you may recognize, such as watching too much TV late into the night, which sabotaged his getting up in the morning, as well as getting distracted by unnecessary emails and web surfing that swallowed up his quiet time. He also found that he was overscheduling himself socially and engaging in emotional dramas that sucked his attention and caused his behavior to revert to stressful ways of being. After reviewing each habit that kept him locked into patterns of avoidance, I asked, "What does this provide that you think you need?" Very quickly James encountered the fundamental fear that preserves all of our ego habits: discovering we do not exist in the way we thought.

OUR CORE FEAR: "I" MIGHT DISAPPEAR

Describing this primary fear, James said, "I see that my familiar ego game is very close to being up. Who I have spent a lifetime thinking was 'me' is really just a fictional character made up of layers of memories, perceptions, conclusions, and self-images. Right now all of this is transparent, like a ghost that does not fundamentally exist."

While James intellectually knew the concept of "no self," actually experiencing his familiar identity disappearing into the void was another matter entirely. To stay present to this new way of being and open beyond the known felt terrifying. "Now what?" he asked.

WHO ARE YOU BEYOND "ME"?

I encouraged James to just be still and allow the feelings of disorientation, to "sense" into the space at the "end of himself." This can feel like floating or like looking through a porthole into the infinite space of the galaxy. Tears poured down his cheeks as he recognized that his fear existed only because he was identified with the "self" looking through the porthole . . . the vastness in which the whole galaxy appears looks from this vantage point like some annihilating "other." I invited him to see if he could soften and open into this new space as his own being—both the one looking and the one being looked upon. The sense of a separate "me" and a separate vast "galaxy" disappeared, and there was simply infinite space, being, and peace. This more than resolved his fear. It fulfilled his deepest prayer.

One of the reasons I emphasize ego relaxation rather than ego annihilation is to help us not be so afraid to let surrender happen. Dancing close to the void always feels scary to our ego, but once we actually let go, it is quite the opposite. We discover that the one trying to keep fear at bay is not actually our true nature—but the "someone" of our history, clinging to what we know, even though we might be complaining loudly about our patterns and actively trying to change them. At the deepest level, our ego clings to what feels familiar in order to protect against the fundamental terror of dissolving.

The more you can let go, the more you will understand that it is only your self-images that can dissolve, and this is always very good news. This kind of "death" resurrects who you truly are because it opens space inside from which Grace can come alive. Grace always brings forth what you most need. Each time you practice ego relaxation into and through fear, your essential qualities, such as boundless love, joy, strength, clarity, and peace, start to come back online. It will vary in flavor each time you let go. As Hafiz said, "Now that all your worry has proved such an unlucrative business, why not find a better job?"[1]

Even though you find yourself sabotaging what it is you say you most want, do not just marinate in your fear. Wherever you are right now—whether you find yourself anxious about life unfolding in the direction you hope or whether fear feels like a familiar way of being—explore it directly.

INQUIRY **Dissolving the Roots of Fear**

This sequence of inquiry questions provides powerful support to help you harness fear as a gateway to a deeper ground of Grace. If possible, do this with a friend you trust.

Otherwise, journal into the following questions.

What do you fear?

Explore *one* fear at a time. Notice the details, such as how this fear feels in your body, in your heart, and simply as thoughts in the mind. Just let the phenomenon of each fear be contacted with compassionate allowing. If overwhelm arises, use these somatic cues: wiggle your toes, sense your feet on the ground, breathe into the belly, and remember that you cannot die from or be harmed by contacting whatever you find. Meet everything as layers of your mind and remember: *there is nothing that you need to fix, get, or do about it.* Once you have contacted a specific fear, then inquire into the identity of it.

Who does this fear belong to?
You might discover that your fear is a view you picked up from your mother, your father, your culture, your religion, or your schooling. It might not even be yours but something you absorbed along the way. You might notice that your fear belongs to a five-year-old inside who has concluded "I am all alone" as a result of a moment of overwhelm when the support you needed did not seem to be available. Ultimately, fear only persists in relation to a story of a separate someone. Keep cycling through these first two questions for ten minutes, naming fears and seeing who they belong to. Notice the energetic sensations in your body and the feelings, memories, and insights that come. When you have gone as deep as you can, spend another ten minutes exploring the next question.

What's alive in the space beyond you and the fear?
Just keep opening, softening, and allowing your experience to unfold. You might find that your fear starts to evaporate or at the very least loses its negative charge. At some point, you will discover a shimmering presence alive in the space beyond what you thought you were and the thoughts of fear. Trust what unfolds in your own experience and cherish what is revealed. Whatever emerges, lean into it and see if you can surf into a spacious inner terrain that is not bound by thought or history. ~

Learning to face the force of fear and open into, through, and beyond it is incredibly empowering. Grace emerges, perhaps bringing some new insight that helps you navigate the best way forward at work, in your relationships, or on the meditation cushion. Perhaps you just feel calmer, more present, and at peace. The more you find your stride in meeting rather than trying to transcend your fear, the more you can discover that fear has no actual foundation, and Grace has no limit. Now you see that truly, there is nothing to fear. You can relax more substantially into an unshakable presence within and continue on the journey.

3 MELTING THE GRIP OF CONTROL

Gently I weep for my mind,
caught in its illusion of ownership.

Mind, you're not who you think you are.
You're dancing over a pit.

Soon you'll fall through,
and these things you've valued
and collected will be left behind.

My sweet dear, do you understand this,
and if you do, how does your food taste?

LALLA, *Naked Song* (translated by Coleman Barks)

The more you recognize what is alive in the space beyond your thoughts of fear, the more you experience Grace as the unchanging ground of your being. Ego relaxation helps you wake up out of the dream of exile to see that your nightmares have been happening within the deepest love imaginable. Not only is this a great relief, it resolves so much everyday stress and struggle. As the density of your fearful fixations starts to melt, you begin to feel more fluid. Ease, joy, and a natural connectedness to the universe return . . . but only if you are willing to surrender the reins of fear's twin sibling—control.

Since freedom is inherently part of your true nature, it is natural to want some sense of agency, to feel in control of your life. On the ordinary level, we all must do the best we can with the hand of cards we have been dealt, taking full responsibility for our experience and not blaming others for our situation. This means making intelligent choices in our career, our health-care habits, our finances, and our relationships. It means being conscious of what we give our energy and attention to.

Yet consider the fact that you do not get to choose the moment of your birth, your death, who you fall in love with, or when accidents or windfalls happen. Clearly there is a deeper intelligence steering the ship of your life, whether or not you want to admit it.

At the age of sixteen, Ramana Maharshi was overcome by an intense fear of death, triggered by a funeral procession passing by and likely influenced by his father's recent passing. Determined to get to the bottom of his quandary, he lay on the floor and held his breath. Not only did he get past the fear but his ego identity dissolved to reveal his true nature as the eternal Self.

After this awakening, the young mystic left his family home for the temple town of Tiruvannamalai, South India. Eventually, his mother found him living as a simple *sadhu* (ascetic) in a cave on Mt. Arunachala and begged him to return home with her. Ramana replied, "The Ordainer controls the fate of souls in accordance with their destiny. Whatever is destined not to happen will not happen, try as you may. Whatever is destined to happen will happen, do what you may to prevent it. This is certain. The best course, therefore, is to remain silent."[1]

ALIGNING WITH DIVINE WILL

Ramana was not advising his mother to be passive or not take appropriate actions in her life. He was challenging her emotional attachment. Inviting her to surrender the delusion of thinking it is our right to boss the universe around.

To "remain silent" is to cease fighting against the mystery. It is to instead choose to give ourselves back to the origin of our being, bringing our personal will into harmony with the power and intelligence that pulses through our bodies, hearts, and lives with astonishing precision. Lao Tzu articulated this same principle of turning personal will into universal will in the sage advice, "Ride the horse in the direction the horse is going." Interestingly, Ramana's mother ended up staying on the mountain with a small cluster of other devotees and awakening into a profound realization herself. She eventually departed this world in a state of *samadhi* (blissful absorption) in her son's arms. We would all be wiser to accept the fact that God always wins, and it knows best.

UNDERSTANDING THE GRIP OF CONTROL

In the same way that you need to meet the energy and the justifications behind your fear instead of trying to rationalize it away, surrendering deeper into the ground of Grace requires that you understand your mechanisms of control and what causes this grip to persist. Even if your personality is easygoing, every ego contains many layers of control.

Control is completely understandable, considering that we begin human life so helpless, so completely dependent on others to intuit and respond to our every need. The poet William Wordsworth wrote that we come "trailing clouds of glory," and yet we all fall out of Grace into a state of separation, thinking we are contained within the boundaries of our physical form. We experience love, peace, strength, and joy—qualities of our own true nature—as commodities we must get from others. For the young child, this feels terrifying.

When fear is not resolved, our survival instinct progresses to control, coming up with some strategy to make our experience seem more manageable. Instinctively, our body contracts into a gripping posture. Commonly, we pull up in the pelvis, hold our breath, and tense our solar plexus. The neck, shoulders, forearms, and hands tighten. Our heart retracts, and our mind becomes very active. We begin to struggle, exert effort, *do something* to offset feeling so agitated and helpless. We contract into the foundational presumption that drives all of our ego activity: "I am the do-er. It's up to me."

"I AM THE DO-ER. IT'S UP TO ME."

Explore any pernicious stress in your life, and at the root you will find this presumption. This "I" is the identity of our ego, frozen in a moment in time. Thus it feels like a young self. Identifying with its own very limited resources, our young self believes it is the one who has to figure it out somehow and create the safety, get the support, and resolve the trouble. Except often, it cannot. Forgetting we are in and part of the Infinite—the spiritual sons and daughters of the Most High—what inevitably follows is an inner struggle. The best we can do in the first phase of our lives is *suppress* what feels like too much, *grasp* what we hope will resolve our fear, or *leave* our direct experience somehow.

Quickly, we learn what strategies seem to work best to secure the love, approval, and attention of our parents. Over time, this becomes our brand of controlling our inner experience. We control the environment around us so that it feels more soothing. We control others so that whatever good we receive from them keeps coming. It is a patch-up job at best. While our strategies of control help us survive a moment of disconnection, they cost us intimate contact with our own essence.

It is important that we bow to the intelligence of our survival instinct, which drove us to adapt and survive our experience of separation. The ways we learned to control are not wrong, but they are very limiting. Nothing will cut us off from the experience of Grace more than exerting effort to control the show.

REFLECTION **Melting Your Grip of Control**

What has started to bubble up inside as you have been reading this chapter? Perhaps you realize that you learned to control others so they would treat you better by appearing not to need much or being pleasing, but at the expense of being authentically yourself. Perhaps your control was more explicit, and you exerted your will by being assertive, competitive, or quick to take the lead, but cut yourself off from the capacity to receive. Perhaps your control took the form of withdrawal, retreating into an inner world of thoughts and ideas, not really letting anyone penetrate your heart. Perhaps your control took the form of performing, trying to elicit positive feedback to feel secure. Perhaps you learned to preempt solutions to multiple problems before they even arose. Perhaps you tried to control yourself, keeping a lid on your seemingly "unacceptable" parts. Since the creative dynamism of the entire universe flows through us, the way you learned to control will be completely unique to you.

How does the grip of control arise in you?
Take some time to journey into this question for ten minutes or so, either with a friend or by journaling or meditating into the question. Begin by letting the question into your body, and notice your somatic and energetic response—how your body contracts into a grip. Notice the feelings that emerge in response to the question, perhaps anxiety or insecurity or anger, even if they do not seem rational. Notice if memories come or insights reveal themselves. Remember that in ego relaxation, all we need to do is meet the forces of our ego and be there. There's nothing to fix, change, get, or do. With every grip of control that you discover, let the next question help you explore the driving force within it.

What does this habit of control presume?
Any grip of control that does not begin to melt upon contact with loving awareness is being held together by a presumption or belief that holding on is necessary or right. Perhaps it feels that if you let go of control, you will collapse into a puddle and not be able to function in daily life. Perhaps you presume that there is no support other than the effort of your own mind. Perhaps the voices of your ancestors, culture, religion, or schooling pipe up inside, objecting that letting go of control is stupid and will make you vulnerable to being taken advantage of or mistreated.

Perhaps you presume surrendering control means that you will be enslaved by another's dominating ego will, as might have happened in your past with a domineering parent or elder sibling. You are never asked to surrender to another ego. You surrender into a deeper truth, which always liberates everyone it touches.

Whom does the grip of control belong to?
Inquiring through my own mechanisms of control, I have at times encountered a primitive layer of my mind that emerges like a craggy old captain, asserting, "I am the captain of this ship" and instinctively grabbing for control as if tethering his ship to the shore. Underneath this caricature of a defense, which I recognized as an introjection of my father when I was a child, is the fear "I" would

not cope. "I" might collapse, be overtaken by another, or disappear into vapor. It only feels disconcerting on the way toward surrender. Once I have relaxed my identification with a structure of my mind that thinks it is in charge, there is no "I" nor "other," only an endless sea of peace.

If you find flavors of resistance arising as you read this chapter, it likely means that you are getting in touch with something important for you. Ultimately, all of our concerns about melting the grip of control belong to a young self inside who is presuming that Grace is something other than total and complete love. ~

CONTACT THE HELPLESSNESS WITHIN YOUR CONTROL

Melting your grip of control ultimately means learning to stay present and feel the stress and helplessness of the little "me" who believes, *I really am all alone here*, and thinks it is the one who has to make everything happen. Inside this belief is a young self who is trying to exert some control but can't. Feeling overwhelmed with no sense of power over our situation is one of the hardest things for any human being to tolerate. It really is a powerful spiritual practice to learn to just stay there, not doing a single thing, even though it feels like an impossible quandary. Chögyam Trungpa Rinpoche spoke powerfully about how it can feel at this important juncture: "The bad news is that you're falling through thin air, nothing to hang on to, no parachute. The good news is, there is no ground."[2]

This is similar to how learning to dive through the liquid force of a wave in the ocean feels so counterintuitive that your mind is convinced you will be annihilated. However, when you actually dive into the wave and then relax, it is a pleasant surprise. Far from smashing you to pieces, the power of the water rolls over you like a massage. You find yourself deeper in the ocean. The good news is that what you let go into does not have any beginning or ending, and you are already within it, so you cannot crash.

THE GROUND OF GRACE OFFERS TOTAL SUPPORT

Ultimately, control is an ego reaction to feeling disconnected from true ground. As children, we naturally look to others to transmit the support we need, without realizing that we are trying to get it from others' egos, which likely do not have access to true support themselves. Your grip of control melts when you realize you exist within an unshakable presence. This true support is not coming from any personality, is not based in history, and is always here, even when very difficult things are happening. Control melts when you receive the support that has always been here.

Even though early awakening experiences had blessed me with access to subtle states of Grace, until I addressed the roots of control, I rarely felt fully relaxed in my own skin, at home on Earth. I struggled with hypersensitivity, and most of my struggles revolved around issues to do with support. Hence my personality was a specialist in control. Looking back, it is now obvious I had a very "top down" awakening, but I was not yet awake from the ground up. This radically changed after I received and learned to engage regularly in a practice I call the "mountain of presence," which I explain below.

THE TRUE ALTERNATIVE TO COLLAPSE OR CONTROL

The game-changing practice of the mountain of presence came to me one morning when I was sitting on a warm, flat rock on Mt. Arunachala overlooking the ancient Shiva temple in the bustling town below. This sacred mountain was not only beloved by Ramana Maharshi but also an important pilgrimage place for countless sadhus over thousands of years. I spent as much time there as I could in the two years after the cave awakening, which involved complete surrender of every attachment. Whenever I would arrive at a threshold of my capacity to yield, feeling that old grip of control reconstellating, I would pray for help to stay present and relax into what was. I kept hearing a soft inner voice that did not have a name or form, whispering, "Just keep opening, just keep softening, just keep allowing."

One time I said back to that voice, "How much more?" The reply came, "Until your surrender is total!" It reminded me of Daniel Ladinsky's rendering of Hafiz:

> What's the difference between your experience of existence
> and that of a saint?
> The saint knows that the spiritual path
> is a sublime chess game with God
> And that the Beloved has just made such a fantastic move
> That the saint is now continually tripping over joy
> And bursting out in laughter, and saying "I surrender!"
> Whereas, my dear, I am afraid you still think
> You have a thousand serious moves.[3]

I sincerely wanted to give up my thousand serious moves. I saw this was not possible as long as I felt that I had to *get* support somehow, pretend I did not need it, or exert effort to support myself by some familiar means.

RELAX INTO UNSHAKABLE PRESENCE

This new focus emerging in my meditation practice felt like the most loving response to my true need to find deeper stability inside during such a shaky time. It provided an expanded capacity to practice ego relaxation with all that arose, without having to revert to historically based strategies of control. Over time, this practice completely changed the way I experienced being here in this world. It brought greater resilience, deeper presence, and expanded capacity for surrender. It can for you too.

When sharing it with my students, I noticed it producing great benefit even among experienced meditators. It powerfully quiets the mind and supports the heart. This is a practice to engage in often. Enjoy!

MEDITATION **Ground in the Mountain of Presence**

1. Sit somewhere comfortable and quiet, where you won't be distracted.

2. Find the posture that best supports an erect spine, with your neck long and your jaw slightly tucked in. Make sure your hips are evenly positioned, and your feet are on the floor (or in a comfortable lotus). Relax your jaw, and let your tongue touch the roof of your mouth lightly. Let your hands fold one over the other in your lap.

3. Dedicate your practice to the benefit of all beings, in gratitude to All That Is.

4. Bring your awareness to the soles of your feet and receive the ground. Take in the sensation of the chair and all that cradles your body and receive the unarguable support through your senses in the here and now. Receive it on the inhale, and melt down into it on the exhale. If this is difficult, just wiggle your toes slightly or rock your pelvis gently, which will support sensing rather than visualizing.

5. Sensing the ground underneath your feet and the chair underneath your body, consider what lies below the earth you are resting upon. Prior to the rocks, minerals, and water beneath the Earth's crust, see if you can take in the primordial energy arising out of infinite space, which is the ground of all being.

6. Sense that immense power beneath you rising like a vast mountain with no circumference. Feel as if your lower body is part of that mountain, subsumed within it, with the crest of that mountain resting in your deep belly center, a couple of inches below your navel (the *dan tien*, or Kath center).

7. Focus on the breath rising and falling in the deep belly, where the top of the infinite mountain gives you total support to just *be here* and *be still.*

8. When you feel deeply settled and quiet, just let go of any focus and simply rest.

If distractions arise, as they inevitably will at first, do not make them mean anything. Just bring your focus back to sensing the breath in the belly, sitting in a mountain of immense presence. Just relax and rest in silent abiding. ~

If you engage in this meditation practice regularly, you will likely begin to feel your lower body starting to open in a profound new way. You might even feel as if your feet have webs of light that naturally ground downward, receiving the immense *prana* (life force) of the Earth. Yet you will notice that it is not just the physical Earth but the power and presence that *caused* the Earth and everything upon it to arise. Your legs, pelvis, and entire lower body might feel enormous, as if you have a stable base that is completely independent of your past. At first, most people mistake this for a visualization, but actually it is not. The more you sense your feet, the ground under you, and the primordial ground, which causes everything to arise, resting in a mountain is how it *actually feels* within your body. The gripping patterns can melt when you relax out of your mind, down into the living Grace, independent of your history.

INQUIRY **Surrendering to *the* Way**

Now that you have explored your strategies of control and the presumptions that hold them together and have taken some time with the meditation, I invite you to see how it feels when your ego will-full-ness surrenders to willingness. Contemplate this question:

What's it like when you surrender your way for "the way"?

Journal into it, take it with you on a walk in nature, or inquire with a friend. I also highly recommend putting it on your fridge as a daily reminder to help you let control melt so you can be more graceful amidst the ordinary. Let the question ripple through your body, your heart, and your mind. Let it take you on a ride beyond the captain and do-ership! ~

The more you recognize the deeper support that is always here, the easier it becomes to practice ego relaxation, meeting everything you find and letting it be. Over time, the grip of control and all that drives it can begin to melt. While some of the tentacles might take time and practice to fully let go, they do not have to hold you back. As control melts and your true willingness grows, the ground of Grace becomes more real. You will surely begin to see that there is more true support for you to be here, however you are, than you ever imagined.

4 DROPPING THE KNIFE OF JUDGMENT

Once a young woman asked Hafiz, "What is the sign of someone knowing God?" Hafiz remained silent for a few moments and then looked deep into the young person's eyes, then said, "Dear, they have dropped the knife. They have dropped the cruel knife most so often use upon their tender self and others."

HAFIZ, *The Subject Tonight Is Love* (translated by Daniel Ladinsky)

Since surrendering fear and control is by definition being vulnerable, to deepen in ego relaxation we need a nonviolent inner atmosphere. "Dropping the knife" distills one of the most important cornerstones for relaxing into the ground of Grace: the need to disengage from judgment, be it projected or internalized.

Our ego tends to confuse judgment with wisdom. It is not that we should not judge; it is that we usually cannot. *A Course in Miracles* poses that "to judge anyone fairly, we would need to be aware of an inconceivably wide range of factors, past, present, and to come. Also, to be certain there is no distortion in our perception so that our judgment is fair. Who except in grandiose fantasies could claim this for themselves?"[1]

Any taste of Grace reveals that we are literally not separate from each other and all that is. Perhaps you already understand that to attack another, even if just through wielding the sword of your mind, is to attack your Self, eroding your own peace of mind. Perhaps you already take your judgments of others less seriously, checking your hasty assumptions. Most people I meet find it harder to learn to drop the knife when it comes to themselves.

One summer afternoon I was sitting on my deck surrounded by giant redwood trees, drinking tea with a friend who is one of the most accomplished people I know. She shared the devastating impact of some unsolicited advice given by a well-intentioned family member that she couldn't shake off. It was a lengthy, written critique of why she had not landed a long-term relationship, spouting well-meaning advice on what she should do to become a more successful person, in this and other areas of her life. The critique had latched its claws onto my friend's own inner judgment, the place inside where she was most vulnerable. Despite her obvious intelligence, she was under attack from within, fighting off the feeling, *there is something wrong with me, and I must work harder to fix myself,* even though she knew this was not true or fair.

BEWARE THE CRUEL KNIFE OF YOUR SUPEREGO

Whenever we land in this kind of inner violence, it is our superego—otherwise known as the inner critic, judge, or commentator—at work. There are many helpful books today about how to get free from this inner negativity (I highly recommend Byron Brown's *Soul without Shame* and Cheri Huber's *There Is Nothing Wrong with You*). But how does superego judgment affect our receptivity to deeper Grace?

Visualize a psychic condom around your personality structure, compressing the crown of your head with a mucous plug, blocking access to higher states of consciousness. At your base chakra is a knot grabbing onto your libidinal life-force energy and harnessing it against the self. This psychic condom shrink-wraps your consciousness to hold your familiar ego identity in place. (This is actually how it looks energetically. No kidding!)

LIFT THE PROTECTION FOR YOUR EGO

The superego develops by internalizing the messages of good/bad and right/wrong you absorbed from parents, teachers, elders, and authority figures, those whose job it was to train you how to function in the world. It is greatly influenced by what you were praised and punished for as a child. This serves you very well in the first phase of life, when it is important that you learn to look both ways before crossing the street, put clothes on before walking out of the house, and know not to place your hand on a hot stove. However, now that you are ready to relax beyond ego and discover a much more Grace-filled way of being, this kind of inner commentary is no longer needed. Furthermore, it blocks the guidance you need to surf into more subtle inner terrain. The condom must come off!

I am sure you are acquainted with the inner critic: the dualistic, critical, judgmental voice inside that offers a running commentary on how you are doing. Its basic message is that you are "good," "right," or "okay" when you are measuring up to some ideal standard, such as being pleasing, high achieving, or in control, not making any mistakes, getting it right, or being whatever was the "right" way to be according to your early authority figures. The superego judges you as "bad and wrong" when you step out of line, failing to live up to the rules in some way. It does not give you much leeway to be messy, make mistakes, not know the answers, or be vulnerable or out of control. Its solution to most problems is that you should be trying harder. Considering what we have been exploring so far about ego relaxation, it is clear that left unrecognized, this can short-circuit your ability to relax into the ground of Grace.

THE FALSE GUIDE THAT RIPS YOU OFF

The voice of the superego has a kind of puffed-up authority to it, a tone of conviction that it is here for your own good. It hooks onto any fear you have, any place where you might still be a work in progress. It believes that without critical counsel, your primal tendencies—what Freud called the instinctual forces of the id—would run amuck. Ramana Maharshi did not use the psychological term *superego*, but he described this layer of mind as "the thief dressed as the policeman, here to guard the treasure."

Commonly, superego judgment douses us in shame when we fall short of our spiritual ideals, co-opting our spiritual practice.

So often dedicated practitioners on the path sit with me in retreat, confessing how they fail to meditate as often or as deeply as they should. Exploring why usually uncovers shame that after years of practice, their mind still won't quiet down, so they avoid coming to practice. Commonly, advanced students wield the knife against themselves when their old patterns arise, saying, "I should be beyond this. I know better."

The word *should*, delivered with a tight, hard energy, is the superego's defining feature. Worst of all, it is the judgment of "spiritual failure" because the body has developed an illness. This pernicious form of the knife is unfortunately rife in many metaphysical circles.

BEWARE THE SPIRITUALIZED SUPEREGO

The superego dressed in "spiritual" concepts often has us *imitating* being loving, kind, present, and open, trying to fit some image of what an awakened being should look like. This can express as judgments like "awakened people are always nice, accommodating, soft spoken, wear nothing but white, listen only to soft devotional music, don't have money, don't have sex, don't wear lipstick, and never express anger." Who made up these silly rules, which tie us into unnecessary bondage? Authentic awakening is not about *trying* to be kinder, nicer, or sweeter via repressing our animal humanity with its instinctual urges. Why try to become something that your true nature already is?

I am sure you agree that it is a basic human right for everyone to be treated with respect and kindness. Just as cleaning an open wound requires the utmost care and gentleness, so practicing ego relaxation through our more vulnerable places to discover a deeper reality requires a strong commitment to kindness for our relative human experience, even though this does not represent the ultimate truth of who you are.

Chögyam Trungpa Rinpoche aptly pointed this out: "Facing yourself is a question of honesty, rather than condemning yourself. Good or bad, the idea is simply to face the facts. Just see the simple, straightforward truth about yourself without cutting yourself down."[2]

EGO RELAXATION IS LOVING *AND* UNCOMPROMISING

We confuse aggressively confronting ourselves with sincere truth telling. Approaching our ego with love usually exposes a fear that we will just pander to our patterns. Our superego counsels that we cannot address bad habits without threats and punitive treatment. This is part of the outdated "macho" approach to awakening by beating yourself into spiritual shape. "Who" thinks "who" needs a beating?

Ego annihilation might have been the traditional way it was done in most ashrams and mystical schools, but then again, up until recently, it was thought that beating your children was right and necessary. Our culture has finally come to see that as unnecessarily brutal. Not only is ego relaxation nonviolent, it is way more efficient. If you were completely honest, would you feel inclined to bring everything into the light of awareness in an environment of judgment or love?

Cultivating a loving inner environment where you can honestly look at yourself is not the same thing as indulging in, wallowing in, or acting out your patterns. It is simply a commitment to be kind with where you are. By accepting that mistakes are an inevitable part of a learning curve, you can turn your primary attention to understanding and surrendering whatever limits your evolution. *Free from dense patterns of your own ego, your life force is free to be of benefit to others.*

JABS OF JUDGMENT EMERGE AS HIDDEN DEFENSES

Inner commentary often cranks up when you are on the threshold of a significant expansion in consciousness, or just after it. Whether stimulated by the judgment of others or judgment that arises like a sharp jab out of nowhere, aggressive inner commentary can pipe up with nasty things like, *I'm such a fuckup, I'm stupid, I'm damaged goods,* or *I'm rotten.* I have seen this expressed by highly functioning people who otherwise seem to have healthy self-esteem: longtime meditators, doctors who save lives, and psychologists with a deep understanding of the human condition.

Since your superego's function is to hold your familiar identity in place, surrendering into subtle terrain beyond a separate "me" represents a significant stepping out of line. This is why as you journey further into Grace, you must learn to spot the knife, understand what it hooks onto, and let it drop. A. H. Almaas, founder of the Diamond Approach, writes in *Work on the Superego*: "Ecstatic or spiritual states usually do not last because, among other things, anxiety or superego attacks return and the defenses reassert themselves, sometimes stronger than before. This happens unless one has learned to tolerate anxiety and dis-engage from the superego. A sound spiritual teaching must therefore include preparation of dealing with the superego."[3]

The following practice is designed to help you drop the knife of judgment, whether it is an overt form of self-attack, a projection onto others, or a looping tape of inner commentary that obscures inner silence.

REFLECTION **Identify Your Superego Triggers**

What kinds of situations most activate the knife of judgment for you? Making mistakes? Not getting it right? Not knowing what to do? Not being proficient at something? Receiving a critique? Disappointing someone you love? Not succeeding with your goals? Being in conflict with another? Feeling weak? Losing your grip in some way? Dropping your "bundle"? Take some time to reflect on the following question:

Where do you feel the most vulnerable, or most unsure, in a learning curve? Your least confident arena is usually the place where you are most vulnerable to a superego attack. Knowing this ahead of time can help you drop the knife more quickly. Instead of feeding the judgment, see if you can turn this vulnerable area into a practice of some kind. If you accept that imperfection is part of being human, then you are free to explore what Grace is asking you to learn, and you can simply start asking for help with it—both in prayer and perhaps from people around you. ~

THE POWER OF NO

During the forty days and nights he spent in the desert, Jesus clearly went through a powerful spiritual purification process in preparation for entering his ministry. He was tempted three times by "Satan," who emerged attacking his approach to the full embodiment of Christhood. This jabbing, nagging voice tempted him to turn stone into bread, throw himself off a cliff and command the angels to catch him, and use his spiritual powers for personal gain. All three temptations were driving him to come off course and violate the purity of his calling. Jesus responded, "Get thee behind me Satan."

Viewing this wonderful story through the lens of gestalt dreamwork, where we view all characters as parts of ourselves, reveals "Satan" as the voice of the superego arising to keep the known reality in check, attacking and jabbing at the approach of an expanded new level. Jesus harnessed the strength of will to say no.

We all need to see our superego activity for what it is and find a way to say no—not to collapse into it, not to get caught up in a fight, and not to rationalize our way out. This does not have to become a war within. Rather, it calls forth our spiritual obedience to a deeper truth.

ACKNOWLEDGE BUT DO NOT FEED: "THANKS FOR SHARING"

Perhaps you have been in a group situation where someone was taking up a lot of airtime. In the same way that you might say, "Thanks for sharing," acknowledging but not feeding their narcissism, you can acknowledge and disengage from something that is not kind or true, whether it is coming from your own mind or another's. You do not have to judge the judgment but simply see the commentary as what *A Course in Miracles* calls "meaningless thoughts." If you feed them, they create meaningless suffering.

This works very well with the running inner commentary that might be trickling through your mind throughout the day. If the inner noise seems to be preventing you from dropping into silence in meditation, playfully set another cushion for "the commentator" to meditate upon, embodying your recognition that it is not the authority here.

Each spring I travel to the Netherlands to lead a retreat at the beautiful Venwoude Institute. Located on the edge of a forest, with a royal residence as the only neighbor, it is home to a community of friends dedicated to waking up in relationship and holding space for others to do the same. Diving deep on retreat, many in the group were struggling to drop the knife of judgment toward themselves. I posed this question: "If you were to walk outside right now and see a man with a hockey stick about to forcefully aggress on a small child, what would you do?"

Everyone agreed that even if the child had been behaving like a spoiled brat, the enactment of such violence would have been damaging to both the child and the adult. Instinctively, you would move to some kind of action to intercept it—perhaps say something, make a startling noise, grab the stick, pull the child out of harm's way. The aggressive judgmental energy you might direct toward yourself to say "I'm such a fuckup" or "I'm damaged goods" is akin to that man with the hockey stick. It warrants any kind of action that intercepts the violence. Different things work for different people.

DIFFERENTIATE THE COMMENTATOR FROM YOUR TRUE HEART

A potent new practice for dropping the knife emerged when I was teaching in Northern Ireland, when Mary asked for help uncovering the root of depression. Mary recognized waves of self-hatred erupting from within her mind to sabotage any attempt at ego relaxation. I asked who the hateful inner voice reminded her of. Mary responded that it was the voices of her childhood priest, her mother, her schoolteacher, and her abusive ex-husband streaming together. Clearly Mary had been on the receiving end of physical, emotional, and spiritual abuse, as is heartbreakingly common. Courageously, Mary was able to stay present and feel the emotional and energetic impact of this conditioning, recognizing how she had absorbed so much hatred and violence and had become attached to it as "right and normal." Together, we just met the layers of suffering, being here, doing nothing so that Grace might find us somehow.

I asked her to tell me a difference between the voice of self-hatred and the truth of her heart. I continued offering her that same question for five rounds. Within minutes, Mary's consciousness palpably began to shift. Tears poured down her cheeks as she said, "I know that this voice that has held me a prisoner of depression for years is not real. I know my heart, which is full of love and peace and beauty, is real. It is holy. This is me."

I asked her how she knew this. She floored me by replying, "Because no one had to teach me this. Despite all these hateful messages of my past, I just know that my heart is uncontaminated. My heart *is* Love."

Mary's suffering and courage birthed one of the most effective tools for dropping the knife I know—I call it a "neutral separation." In the following inquiry practice, we use discriminating awareness to see the difference between the false guide and the heart's truth.

INQUIRY **Discriminate the False from the Real**

I encourage you to try journaling or meditating into this question for at least ten minutes, or until such time as the knife of judgment drops.

Name a difference between the voice of self-attack and the truth of your heart.
For example: My self-attack is hard and punitive, and my heart is soft and naturally accepting. My self-attack is the voices of the past, and my heart is not bound in time. My self-attack is black and white, and my heart naturally spacious.

It does not matter what differences you find. It is more the process of sifting the egoic from the essential that brings liberating Grace alive. Simultaneously, it directs your attention to the truth of your heart. When we contact a layer of the heart deeper than our changing emotions, it is very obvious what is and is not real. ~

RECLAIM YOUR VITAL ALIVENESS WITH HUMOR

When you feel the energy of attack bearing down upon you, and when saying, "No, thanks for sharing" or practicing the neutral separation question is not sufficient, it is likely that your life-force energy needs to be reclaimed. Since the superego harnesses your own libidinal energy, this often needs to be liberated from the clutches of the fake authority. This is the time to engage in something wacky, offbeat, and energetic in the service of your humanity.

In a safe space where no one else is around, try stringing together all of your favorite swear words. (Yes, go on, and don't be polite.) Say them as fast as you can, with as much enthusiasm as possible. Really let it rip, and then let your body get into it with something vigorous, perhaps a dance, wringing a towel, beating the cushions on your sofa, or shaking your whole body as vigorously as you can for a minute or so. This is likely to feel weird at first, but embrace weird and just see what happens. Most people burst out laughing fairly quickly, the inner negativity lifts, and one's juicy aliveness returns. This usually does the trick for enabling one to drop that knife.

CHANGE THE CHANNEL WITH DEVOTION

Just as you might change the channel on your TV when you are no longer enjoying the show, engaging mantras or prayers as part of your practice can be a powerful support to simply shifting gears inside. As part of dropping the knife, it is always a good idea to open into the realms of being that are never bound or limited by any history. There is way more help at hand than you realize. Turning your consciousness into any name of God or enlightened being that you relate to and asking for help or saying a mantra that has been intoned by millions of beings before you carries immense power to shift your consciousness from the density of judgment to spacious loving presence. Whether you turn into a known *mukti* (liberation) mantra like Om Namah Shivaya, which means, "I bow to the Absolute; please dissolve my ignorance," or the metta prayer, which appears below and I wrote about extensively in my first book, *Boundless Love*, you are becoming divinely disobedient to the distortions of judgment. Devotion is giving your allegiance to the reality of the heart, calling its love forward. This chant and many others are available on my mantra CD, *The Heart of Being*, available via mirandamacpherson.com.

> *Metta Prayer*
> May all beings dwell in the heart.
> May all beings be free from suffering.
> May all beings be healed.
> May all beings know their wholeness.
> May all beings be happy and at peace.

When you really need compassion, prayers like this give your mind a place to fold into when the judgment is too loud. Not only will it help to settle the mind but it will also activate the deeper heart and bring forward its qualities of love, compassion, and kindness for all, which cannot coexist with the knife of judgment.

YOU ARE NOT A PROBLEM TO BE FIXED

Please read that again, slowly: you are not a problem to be fixed. The superego is always pointing out your faults and telling you how to fix them; yet no matter how hard you try, how much you compensate, it is never enough. On closer investigation, the movement to fix yourself is an expression of self-hatred. It reifies the confusion that it is your ego that needs to improve and get enlightened. This is not true or even possible.

Ego relaxation calls you to surrender the powerful urge to try to fix yourself, even by spiritual means. Learning to be as you are—as a relative human being in a process of growing, learning, and awakening *and* as eternal changeless being—you discover that there never has been anything wrong with you. You remain in and part of the Divine, where you have been all the time. Refusing to yield the knife of judgment against yourself, or anyone else, means you are no longer held back from deepening into the ground of Grace. You begin to feel the unchanging support that helps melt the dense forces of fear, control, judgment, and defensiveness. This prepares you to receive a new dimension of Grace, one that brings luminous states to fill your inner cup, exponentially.

PART II

RECEIVING THE BLESSINGS OF GRACE

The winds of Grace are always blowing,
It is for us to raise our sails.

Often attributed to SRI RAMAKRISHNA

In part 1, we explored Grace as the primordial ground of our being. Recognizing that we exist within and as part of an unshakable presence makes it possible to practice ego relaxation—surrendering beyond the dense forces of fear, control, and judgment to gain access to our hidden depths.

While the ground of Grace feels like a mountainous universal presence rising up to support you being present and undefended, the blessings of Grace feel very intimate, as though you are being personally touched by what Rumi calls "an unseen presence we honor, that gives the gifts."[1] It can feel like being in a cosmic shower of divine love, light, and refined nectars that truly quench your thirst.

This dimension of Grace is exquisitely attuned, meeting you in the place of your deepest need, expressed in the biblical saying, "Indeed, the very hairs on your head are numbered."[2] In Vedic cosmology, the deity Vishnu personifies this dimension of the Divine, providing infinite sustenance to the sincere aspirant. Even traditions such as Tibetan

Buddhism that do not emphasize the concept of a Supreme Being offer countless practices to receive the blessings of *bodhisattvas* (beneficent beings who exist in subtle realms to assist in your awakening).

Receiving the blessings of Grace fills you from within and reminds you that every second of life is a gift. Blessings often arrive as synchronicity, where you seem to be in precisely the right place at the right time to meet your life partner, discover an unexpected opportunity in your career, or happen upon a teacher or spiritual guide who seems tailor-made to unlock your inner doors.

It is Grace that gifts you with your children and even with the challenges that arrive on your doorstep; both are sent to grow you. Grace is also ordinary and everyday—uplifting you through great art, wrapping you in the warmth of laughter with a good friend, or piercing you open with the exquisite beauty of morning birdsong. All arrive as gifts from beyond your ego's effort.

More than anything, the blessings of Grace help you accept the fact that you are inherently loved and valued, not because of what you have achieved but just because you exist. In the handful of times that I have sat with someone in their dying process, close to entering the death state, they have uttered, "There is so much love." Divine love is very real, as long as we do not make demands of how it "should" manifest.

These next four chapters invite you to enter into the receptive state of Grace—through trust, humility, patience, and joy. Not only do these virtues make ego relaxation easier, they powerfully refine and elevate your consciousness, ushering you into subtle states of Grace. This ends the spiritual poverty of lack, resolves struggle, and helps you relax and enjoy the gift of life.

5 CULTIVATING TRUST

All is well,
And all shall be well,
And all manner of things shall be well.

JULIAN OF NORWICH,
fourteenth-century Christian mystic and theologian

Diving inward to retrieve the jewel of our true nature calls for great courage. Sometimes the spiritual path lights us up with inspiration, filling our hearts with love, joy, and beauty. Then at other points, we are asked to let go of everything we know and everything we thought we were and to allow all that is familiar to dissolve. Letting go of just one habit or one way of knowing ourselves can initially feel terrifying. This is why every spiritual tradition emphasizes the importance of cultivating deep trust. Trust is what gives us the courage to open into the unfamiliar without defending, collapsing, or controlling. In this way we reclaim chambers of Grace that have been lying dormant within our deep being.

As my life in the United Kingdom came to a close after fifteen years, inner guidance was nudging me toward the United States, and specifically to the San Francisco Bay area—a place I had never been and where I knew no one. Having allowed such a deep surrender of all the structures that had held my known identity in place, I had come too far to lead from fearful caution. Inwardly I asked of the deep silence, *What wants to be received? What wants to be known? What wants to be done?* And I listened for the next step. I was devoted to embodying the truth that had come freshly alive within my heart and wanted the grounding structures of this new life to genuinely support that. It called for a totality of trust while walking moment by moment into the unknown.

The guidance about the next step always came, but only one piece at a time. This meant I had to live and act radically attuned to the pulse of truth in the moment—a brilliant training now that I look back on it. Standing in the immigration line at John F. Kennedy airport was a vulnerable moment. In post 9/11 America, I bore the suspicious label of "alien," and as such, after a long sleepless flight was forced to stand with others of my kind in pens like cattle. The atmosphere was airless and thick with suspicion.

I had been traveling the world fulfilling teaching commitments, coming in and out of the United States on a tourist visa for almost a year while my working visa was in process. Now that my divorce was finalized, I no longer had a home in England, and I had left my native Australia as a young woman of twenty-one. Technically, I was homeless and stateless. Standing in that long immigration line, I knew there was no guarantee I would be let into the country on a tourist visa. I had no plan B. My legs felt like jelly under me. There was no denying the vulnerability of my situation. While waiting for what felt like hours, I had to find a way to turn this into some kind of practice.

I decided to breathe, soften, open, and allow even this—an experience of great uncertainty at the mercy of a giant impersonal bureaucracy. What could I trust? I had no control over what would happen, and at that time I was coming to the limit of my capacity to live out of a suitcase with no fixed abode. I really needed to feel some ground under me. I needed a country. I trusted the guidance that had brought me to this place, but would the US immigration department work off the same circuit as my guidance?

Standing in that line, there was nothing I could do but take the next step, in body and in consciousness, and trust in the deeper plan. If it were "true" for me to begin a new life here in the United States, it would happen. If this were not the deepest truth, then whatever that turned out to be, I would surrender to it. I found myself praying to the "soul" of the United States, just offering up the truth of my own heart—my need for a home and also my dedication to be a loving, positive presence to this land and its people. I had no control over the *how*. By the time I reached the counter of the immigration clerk, I was simply present, meeting another human being on the other side of the desk, just another face of the same mystery, fulfilling his appointed function in this life. Although I had walked though such immigration lines meeting that same tense atmosphere countless times, when it came down to it I had always glided through. The hand of Grace, once again, had taken care of things.

The deeper we trust, the more easily we can open to the new—whether that means spiritually opening to a new dimension we do not yet understand or allowing change in our life situation. Trust is the antidote to fear that gives us the confidence that it is *okay* to open up and let go. Trust gives us strength and courage to walk the path deeply, challenging our automatic responses even when we feel vulnerable and don't know the way. Trust is the muscle we need to continue relaxing control and allowing a deeper intelligence to guide our path in life.

Trust is our creative power to anchor to either fear or to the nourishing love of existence for itself. The deeper our trust, the more exponentially we can surrender in ego relaxation. This makes us more receptive to guidance beyond the historical patterning of our mind. *A Course in Miracles* names trust as the central characteristic of the teacher of God. Not only does it help us relax into a "basic trust" of life, it is also a gateway to receiving subtle blessings beyond ordinary conception.

TRUST IN WHAT EXACTLY?

Although my move to a new life and continent turned out well (way better than anticipated actually!), we cultivate trust not so that life will always unfold according to our desires but rather so that whatever happens, we can relax and trust that things will work out for the best. We cultivate trust first in the goodness of our own true nature rather than our ego's learned strategies of defense. We cultivate trust that this same goodness resides in everything and everyone, even though in many, it is buried and distorted. With practice we discover that placing our trust in this goodness within others can evoke it (I will speak more on this in chapter 16). Most importantly, we cultivate trust that the pulse of existence itself is beneficent. Dante referred to it this way: "The loving goodness has such wide arms that it welcomes whatever turns to it."[1] We cultivate trust that life moves in the direction of liberation, and we are given what we need to evolve and thrive, even when the packaging is hard for us to appreciate.

TRUST DOES NOT DENY DIFFICULTIES

How can we trust the loving goodness underlying all existence when life also includes such difficult things? Life contains death, sickness, disappointment, unexpected tragedy, and expressions of deep cruelty. It can be hard to trust when we see that people often do not treat one another well, we don't always get what we want, and natural disasters and difficult things happen that we do not understand. It is important that we not confuse trust with naïveté in order to avoid facing our difficulties and responding intelligently to life's challenges. It is wise to lock your front door, not leave valuables on display in your car, and make intelligent financial plans for the future. The trust we need is not blind trust.

Like the atmosphere that unconditionally allows both trees and pollution, the invitation to trust points to something deeper than the polarities of good and bad that manifest in this world, something even more unconditional that underlies duality altogether. Life contains many mysteries that from our ego awareness we cannot possibly always grasp. Trust invites us to remember that even when we do not understand why or how, life is trying to evolve us. Both joyful and difficult experiences can birth deeper wisdom if we can inquire sincerely and open into the invitations they contain.

TRUST ACCORDING TO OUR EGO

It's not that we ever really lack trust but more that we tend to trust in our ego's view of reality, which is inherently fearful. From a position of separation, our ego absorbs difficult facts of life into evidence that confirms there is no loving goodness to relax into. This evolves into a view that we really are alone and therefore must tighten up and control in the way we learned when we were young. When we identify with our separation from loving goodness, life seems chaotic and random, and we inevitably conclude we may as well just narrow our circle of concern and take care of our "self" and a few chosen friends or family.

This "reality" according to our ego assumes we are separate from the love, support, and holding we need. It assumes that we are indeed limited to the faculties of our mind and body, and that the best chance of survival we have is to control, suppress, deny, project, and contract to keep ourselves safe from a hostile external world. These become the basic assumptions that govern our lives. Until we recognize that we are looking at the world through a distorted lens, our trust in these tenets is absolute, and our contracted ego patterns are held firmly in place.

TRUST AND OUR EARLY ENVIRONMENT

Our relationship with trust begins when we are infants and is greatly influenced by the quality of "holding"—physically, emotionally, practically, and spiritually—that we felt in the first few years of life. As babies, we are incredibly sensitive and are naturally building beliefs about how the world is, based on how we are being responded to. Our relationship to trust is especially influenced by how we felt we were mothered as infants. Unless you had an enlightened being for a mother, there were likely moments in which your mother was not perfectly consistent, not attuned to your needs at this tender time when you could not even speak them, or not radiating her presence as calm and loving.

In the best-case scenario, your mother (or mothering figure) was well supported, not too stressed, in touch with her own heart, and naturally able to intuit and respond in a loving way to your needs. In the worst-case scenario, your mother was stressed by any number of financial, practical, relational, psychological, or physical circumstances or had received inadequate holding herself. These are the kinds of factors that often give rise to a mother who is "cut off," neglectful, incompetent, cold, hard, or abusive. Where this has been the case, it is especially valuable to find experienced support in order to digest these early experiences. It is completely understandable that we form beliefs early on about how safe the world is, whether or not it is okay to just be as we are, the likelihood of something bad happening if we try something new, and whether we are supported inherently.

Trust is so imperative to our capacity to open spiritually that, on longer retreats, I often begin by inquiring into our relationship with trust using the question, "What limits your capacity to trust?" In an atmosphere of complete permission to meet whatever arises, we allow the exact challenges that cause us to assume we are not safe to be seen, felt, and understood without commentary. Perhaps you could sit with this question right now. What limits your capacity to trust?

MISTRUST ARISES FROM PAST HURTS

Give space for whatever comes in response to asking, "What limits your capacity to trust?" even though it might not seem logical. Hurts from the past can arise—moments when you were on the receiving end of neglect, unkindness, harshness, or lack of understanding or support. You might contact sadness, hurt, or anger that is still lodged in your soul from these experiences. You may remember moments in which something difficult happened and support was not there. Practicing ego relaxation means just staying present and contacting whatever you find without judging or justifying your experience. There is nothing you need to do but be with the question and meet your authentic response.

You may encounter beliefs absorbed from your parents, your culture, or your religion, such as "Wait for the other shoe to drop," "You can only rely upon yourself," or "The world is scary and unsafe."

You might meet nonconceptual patterns of fear, stress, and tension arising from your body. These are often the energetic imprints from overwhelming moments during which you held your breath and closed down to get through a difficult experience. What arises is always very personal to your history, and it is important to just let it come to light rather than try to skip over it. Most importantly, as we saw in the previous chapter on dropping the knife of judgment, it is vital not to criticize yourself for whatever you find but instead practice with compassion for your humanity.

TRUST AND THE REJECTION OF LOVE

Sometimes, in our deepening spiritual journey, we bump into a layer of hatred for the light or hatred for anyone who speaks of love, God, beneficence, or goodness. You would not be alone if you started to feel enraged by all this talk of loving goodness. Sometimes hurt and pain cut so deep that we can't tolerate talk of something we need so much but feel is denied to us. This can easily cause you to trash and reject the voice for love or hide out in cynicism or declare yourself an atheist. If that arises as you inquire into the limits of your capacity to trust, just let it arise without judging yourself or trying to justify why you feel that way. Just see what is there and remember that ego relaxation means you don't need to *do* anything about it. To paraphrase Carl Jung, awareness itself is curative.

The good news is that the tendency to trust in your ego's view of reality is a learned response. Fearful patterns were learned, so they can be unwound. Just as the body's intrinsic homeostatic mechanism can heal a broken bone with the support of a plaster cast, so your soul contains this homeostatic program. When given good support, it knows how to dissolve what is not primordial to your authentic being. You can learn to trust in something deeper than your past, and with this a whole new possibility can open.

ENGAGE WITH PRESENT GOODNESS

Cultivating trust is like building a particular kind of spiritual muscle—one that develops when you consciously recognize and lean into whatever present goodness you contact. This is an important discipline. Rather than automatically letting your mind run away with assuming that things will unfold as they may have in the past, you can practice shifting your attention away from replaying "evidence" for mistrust to inquiring, "What's holding you now?" This shifts your focus from flushing out the hurts of the past to exploring what you might have been overlooking in the present.

Stressful ego patterns usually revolve around a story from the past in which you felt disconnected from loving holding. Yet such fears can be intercepted when you turn your attention toward recognizing what is actually here in the present. This is a discipline of staying in the here and now, committed to not looping back into referencing memory. Consider this: Right now you are likely sitting on a chair or couch or perhaps positioned with your feet upon the ground. Notice the points of contact between your body and the chair or the floor and take in the *fact* of this present holding. Notice how it feels to you. Consciously receive it as an expression of love.

WHAT'S HOLDING YOU NOW?

Notice that you naturally draw in air, containing life-giving oxygen. Notice that you did not have to earn this, nor exert effort to receive it. Furthermore, if you look out the window, you might see some plant life—providing beauty, inspiration, shade, and oxygen to sustain your life. At the most basic level, even if you have had a very difficult history, there is no denying the fact that there exists a basic holding for your being that is unconditional right now. It lets you be here exactly as you are.

In this moment there are whole monastic communities praying for you and your well-being. This is love coming toward you from people you may never personally meet, who are actively wishing you peace and happiness. What if you received these words on the page coming alive as a loving holding to wrap around you as a presence that cares and wants the best for you? What if everything you see, hear, and touch is not just inanimate material but dynamically alive and infused with the boundless love of existence for you? Consider that loving presence itself is extending nourishment to you through every sight, sound, and touch you encounter in this moment.

What if every being who ever realized their true nature—from Buddha to Christ, to the *rishis* (seers) of India and the sages of all the traditions—actively exists within the same atmosphere that you exist within? Whether you believe or don't believe, consider the possibility that loving support is here for you in the present moment. Whether it works for you to call on an inner teacher, guru, name of the Divine, or the presence of someone you have experienced as deeply accepting and kind, lean toward the evidence that supports a sense that there is some holding here . . . and that you do not have to *do* the holding, nor work to hold yourself. Whatever your difficult history and whatever your reasons are to trust only in your fearful habits, you can tone this spiritual muscle, and like any other, it will grow stronger and in a direction that genuinely supports your liberation.

OPEN TO LIMITLESS HOLDING

Within every spiritual tradition of the world, often de-emphasized but not absent, is a personification of the loving dimension of the universe expressing as the Divine Mother. In Buddhism she is Tara, the bodhisattva of compassion, existing specifically to liberate all beings from the eight fears. In Hindu culture, she is the Grace who takes many forms of love, from the most luminous Lakshmi to the most fierce Kali. In Christianity, she is Mary, the mother of the Christ presence, and Sophia, the font of wisdom. In Judaism, she is Shekinah, the indwelling spirit of nonabandoning love, who provides a bridge to our true home. She is Gaia, the Mother Earth, unarguably a living being that graciously holds us, nurtures us, and gives us a home. All cultures independently have personified this dimension of the Absolute, which is dynamic, loving, and holding—the kind that never leaves regardless of the density of our knots.

As I worked through some very challenging ego patterns in my twenties, of self-hatred, of feeling unworthy and without value, I found myself instinctively taking the most contracted parts of my mind to the holding of the Divine Mother. Intuitively I knew that there were parts of my psyche that just could not relax and unwind without a certain kind of holding. Praying, chanting mantras, and asking for help with things I was caught in had a powerfully soothing impact on my nervous system and supported my capacity to let go of some painful stories. I wrote about this extensively in my book *Boundless Love*. It helped enormously to know that despite my history, there was a quality of unconditional holding available that I could turn toward and relax in.

Try the following meditation and inquiry practices, and see if you can turn toward and relax in unconditional holding.

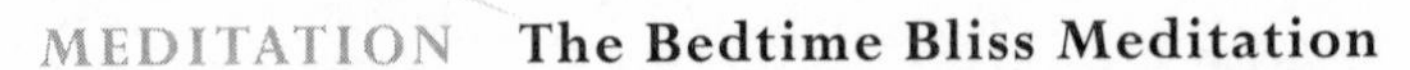

MEDITATION **The Bedtime Bliss Meditation**

Since the ordinary act of going to sleep each night is a kind of surrender into the mystery, it is a perfect opportunity to receive the loving presence that makes us more robust. It also optimizes the nourishing rejuvenation of deep restful sleep. I recommend that this simple practice become part of your daily life.

1. As you approach your bed, give thanks for the blessing of having basic shelter and a comfortable place to rest tonight—and wish that for all beings.

2. Peel back the covers and slip into bed, laying your body on the mattress and pillow in the way that feels best to you.

3. Sense the delicious sensation of the sheets against your skin and the soft cradling of the mattress and bedding and consider the possibility that everything you are sensing is more than what it seems.

4. Consider the possibility that everything you touch is infused with infinite loving holding that softly cradles you with the precise qualities you truly need.

5. As your body becomes heavy, feel a delicious letting go into your pillow, mattress, and bedding as though melting into a sea of infinite soft light—the presence of the Divine Mother herself, which is independent from any person from your history. She is the unending sea of all sustenance.

6. Let go into deep rest, held within an infinite and spacious embrace. ~

INQUIRY **Cultivating Trust**

This inquiry into trust and holding is especially important if you struggle with anxiety or with letting go of the familiar or have difficulty with change.

While all of the inquiries in this book can be used as a reflective meditation to journal into, this one is best done with a friend you trust—since most of our mistrust is formed in relationship. Set a timer for at least ten minutes, and have someone ask you these questions, with plenty of space to let them reverberate through your body, speaking to whatever might be happening in your somatic experience. Also, let the questions into your heart, and speak to whatever feelings, emotions, or memories arise. Additionally, see what awareness and insights come. The more detail you can let come forward, the more your consciousness will open up.

What limits your capacity to trust the loving goodness underlying your life?
When you and your friend have each had a turn with this question, move to the following lines of inquiry for fifteen to twenty minutes.

What's holding you now?
See what comes, and then let it go further with the next question.

What's this holding like, in body, heart, and mind?
If you reach a point where you feel "I have answered the questions" and think you are done, I highly recommend that you keep going for a little longer. The point where you feel you have nothing more to say is usually where true inquiry beyond your mind begins! ~

The more you notice what is holding you and consciously receive it—from the most basic evidence for love to the subtlest levels of loving light—the more trust grows. You will find that your body relaxes down into the belly, viscerally perceiving the goodness of just being here on Earth. Your heart can open to feel the fact of love that can express itself through your human relationships but is not limited to having to come through anyone. Your mind can literally drink in divine love, which feels like being in a refined shower of luminous golden light that is always raining down upon you, just as the sun shines its rays upon the Earth. Taking in the loving goodness and learning to trust it is singularly one of the simplest but most powerful ways to support the flourishing of your heart, mind, and life. Trust provides the platform for a deeper surrender into the mystery.

6 HUMILITY

Bowing to the Mystery

Be still, and lay aside all thoughts of what you are and what God is,
All concepts you have learned about the world,
All images you hold about yourself.
Empty your mind of everything you think is true or false, good or bad.
Hold on to nothing.
Do not cling to one belief you learned before about anything.
Just come with wholly empty hands unto God.

Adapted from *A Course in Miracles: Workbook for Students,* lesson 189

Recognizing what's really holding you and learning to trust it helps you relax out of the past, into love's presence. Not only does this unleash greater ease and happiness, it provides a springboard to dive beyond your concepts of what you are and what the world is. Humility opens the gate, beckoning you to come and drink from the inner fountain of the mystery.

You only have to look at a photograph of the Dalai Lama, Nelson Mandela, or Ramana Maharshi to behold the beauty of a human being devoid of the puffiness of pride. Every wisdom tradition acknowledges humility as the fragrance of a mature soul and as a virtue that supports surrender. Further still, humility can usher you into the celestial state of Grace, where you are spontaneously available to receive subtle nectars beyond the sense of "me" and "my."

HUMILITY RESOLVES THE PROBLEM OF PRIDE

Pride makes our soul opaque and closed to receiving the blessings of Grace. However, there is such a thing as "healthy pride." Intuitively, we know how important it is to give positive mirroring to our children, affirming their qualities and capacities, so they develop inner confidence and self-respect. On an ordinary level, there is a deep satisfaction that comes from giving our best and doing anything well, be it cooking a gourmet meal, mastering a musical instrument, or completing a project. Even enjoying the warm glow of appreciation for honing our skills need not become a spiritual problem if we recognize the gifts placed within us are not to our personal credit.

I am sure you, dear reader, are not an obviously prideful person, going about your day bragging, self-aggrandizing, and aggressively competing to beef up a flaccid self-esteem. Yet the way of Grace invites you beyond the goal of positive psychology. This is not about getting a spiritually improved version of your personality, minus the parts you do not like. I am inviting you into gnosis—direct mystical knowing of who you truly are, what truly *is*.

Tasting Grace challenges the subtle pride of trying to navigate through life from the vantage point of the historically based "me." Not only is this a very stressful, limited way of being, but it contains an unconscious arrogance that denies the fact that every one of us is being lived and breathed by a mysterious presence so much more intelligent than our mind. Yet even for the spiritually seasoned, it can feel very edgy to "come with wholly empty hands unto God."[1]

WHAT IS TRUE HUMILITY?

It is easy to hear the transmission of ego relaxation that asks us to "be nothing, become nothing" as a negating put-down rather than an exquisite yielding back into the Source of our being. Initially, it can feel like being asked to sacrifice all that makes life fun. All too often, conventional religions have promoted the loosening of ego pride by a harsh doctrine of self-sacrifice, even affirming in Catholic liturgy "I am not worthy to receive." Sadly, this has blocked so many from entering into the receptive condition, not to mention caused significant confusion as to what humility really is.

True humility does not ask you to bat away compliments or acknowledgment when it comes; it asks only that you do not use them to inflate. Humility does not demand that you live in austerity, denying enjoyment of life's sensual pleasures; it asks only that you watch the tendency to make material possessions a false idol. Humility is not mimicking the gestures of your spiritual heroes; it is remembering that you exist because of something so much greater than "I."

BEING HUMBLED BY LIFE

Life has a way of popping our pride. Whether they come knocking on your door in the form of a cancer diagnosis, a demotion, a divorce, or the loss of your social standing, challenges to your carefully manicured self-image never feel like blessings at first. It feels as if things are going terribly wrong. Yet if we can surrender into the situation and accept its invitation to empty out, it somehow becomes the very crucible that most liberates us.

This was the case for my dear, late friend Andy, when a false accusation by an angry former patient stripped him of his money, most of his friends, and his status as one of New York's top physicians. I will never forget walking the dog together one spring afternoon in Central Park. He looked up at me while scooping his Labrador's poop into a plastic bag and said, "Prison was the best thing that ever happened to me. I had become so prideful, so fake." He was equally as graceful in the five years afterward, journeying consciously toward the end of his days with leukemia. He died a free man, at peace with himself.

Likewise, Sarah, a powerful CEO in the peak of her career, embraced a breast cancer diagnosis as an invitation to let go of everything that was not working in her life, which meant honestly facing the places she had become tough, disconnected from her own tender heart and its knowing. Today, her radiance is astonishing, and she speaks freely about "the gift of cancer." The more we humbly embrace the cards that life has dealt us, the more they have the power to transform us.

HUMILITY HELPS YOU EMPTY OUT

We saw in chapter 3 how stress and struggle unfold from believing, "I am the do-er." Left unchecked, this develops into a lack of humility in the face of the mystery, presuming "I know" or "I should know." Trying to lead yourself into deeper spiritual waters from within your story of being a separate someone is what causes the spiritual struggle.

Humility relaxes this falsity in an instant by inviting you into the receptive purity of "being nothing." It is not a negation but a quiet settling in which you naturally become intimate with the living intelligence that birthed every one of us into existence. It is because of this living mystery that you are reading the words on this page and drawing breath right now. It is what has known you and loved you all the days of your life. You are never out of its operation.

Humility invites you to recognize that you are not who you have taken yourself to be. You are way deeper. The world and everything within it is way more exquisite and more dimensional than your physical eyes might perceive. Accessing mystical vision demands you to step back from the pride of "I know" and empty out, beginning by emptying out your presumptions. Not just the judgments, projections, and opinions that obviously cause trouble but also your presumptions of what the world is, even what you believe to be true spiritually. Without emptying your mind of what Zen practitioners call "yesterday's rice," you cannot receive the blessings, gifts, and nourishment you need for today. Let the following reflection open some more space inside.

REFLECTION **Opening Up Space for Grace**

Right now, take a few deep breaths and look around you, considering freshly whatever your eyes light upon—perhaps the view onto trees or familiar objects like furniture, plants, or even the flesh of your own hand. Reflecting upon whatever you see, can you honestly say you understand what you perceive? That you are seeing it objectively? That you know it?

Perhaps you recognize that layers of presumption and conditioning influence everything you see. For example, when you were a young child, someone pointed to objects in the environment and gave you a label for them—*tree, book, hand*—that you likely repeated after them. This entrainment patiently provided by your elders taught you how to navigate the world. Yet once things are labeled, they are absorbed into our interior platform for reality as a given. We then continue building upon what we already know. Rarely do we consider anything freshly from our original presumption.

I invite you to just be with whatever your eyes light upon. Consider the possibility that you do not really "know" it. You might not even understand it. What else is here if you do not take your presumption to be the reality? ~

HUMILITY IS NOT HUMILIATION

I have yet to meet someone who did not have to unlearn the tendency to cover over what they do not know. Our ego tends to feel a sense of humiliation, deficiency, and shame in admitting, "I don't know." This usually relates to the classroom of our childhood. Things are slowly evolving in the way we educate our young, but the dominant model for many of us was a linear approach to memorizing and then regurgitating preexisting knowledge. This can be very helpful for learning multiplication tables and good grammar, but it cannot navigate us into the subtle depths that require us to "hold on to nothing."

Reflecting on your relationship with "I do not know," consider what might have happened if you just said this out loud as a child. Sadly, few people report feeling this would have been okay past the age of seven. Perhaps you felt intense pressure to get the "right" answer to the question your teachers posed and avoid being regarded as stupid, or worse still, punished or ridiculed for not knowing. If you have any hangovers of humiliation from your schooling experience, I encourage you to continue reading this chapter slowly, with particular kindness. Then reread it again and be sure to do the exercises!

Peeling back the sense of humiliation for not knowing is crucial; otherwise it will hold together the subtle pride of presuming "I know," continuing to cover your ego's limitations. This results in trying to lead yourself from within an out-of-date navigation system, mentally head-butting your way through life. If you sincerely want to receive the blessings of Grace, you must give up trying to direct your own awakening process. Your ego cannot get enlightened.

BEFRIENDING THE POWER OF "I CAN'T"

Entering the receptive state of Grace requires you to befriend the empty spaces, to make friends with the mystery. This begins with accepting it is totally okay when you do not know the answer or do not even know who you really are. If you want your life to blossom into a work of art, admitting that you do not know is a requirement.

Humbly acknowledging the truth of "I can't do it; I do not know the way" without collapsing opens the energetic knot of pride in the subtle body at the top of the head. If you do not entertain any shame about this, it ushers you into the receptive state, where your mind is not bound by thought or past perception.

It can feel like you are settling into the soft, vast, black silence of the void—being nothing and no one. This is a world away from ego flagellation or putting yourself down. It is deeply vulnerable, but surprisingly peaceful. All stress disappears.

STRETCHING INTO INNER SPACE

Consider the last time you spent the night somewhere new and had to navigate to the bathroom and then back to bed in the middle of the night without turning on the lights. When you cannot navigate from the memory of familiar placement of your own home, perhaps you slow down and sense into the dark space ahead of you, feeling your way. While you might go slower, if you relax into the dark emptiness rather than tense up and try to remember where things are, somehow *the way* finds you.

This can give you a feel for stretching into the unfamiliar spaces inside, without referencing thought or history as the guide. You do not have to know how. You do not have to collapse in shame about that. You do not have to contract—just soften, open, and stretch into the soft, dark spaces at the edge of "I can't; I do not know." Lorin Roche's translation of the Vijnana Bhairava Tantra illustrates the idea of softening into "I don't know" without shame, perfectly:

> You are stunned, powerless.
> You thought you knew
> What was going on.
> Now you realize you don't have a clue.
> You are stopped in your tracks.
> Everything within your skin is shaking.
> Enter this shaking.
> Get curious.
> Look around inside with wonder.
> Unwind your mind.
> All the walls have fallen down—
> Go ahead and dissolve.
> The One Who Has Always Been,
> Who has seen much worse than this,
> Is still here.
>
> **LORIN ROCHE,** *The Radiance Sutras*[2]

Perhaps even reading these words you begin to feel a soft, stepping back inside to a vast silent spaciousness. Like a magnet will draw iron shavings toward itself, this draws you into right relationship with your Source and the rest of life. It purifies your consciousness, helping you be found, ever freshly, by a Grace deeper than your mind.

OPENING INTO THE CELESTIAL STATE OF GRACE

One of the greatest blessings of my life came after I was powerfully humbled through a brutal and very public divorce. It stripped me of my social standing, all but a few friends, my support system, and pretty much every attachment that was holding up my familiar identity. Once I prayed in the middle of the night: "Help me to understand what the invitation is here, so I can say yes to it." In the silence of my meditation, I heard that same voice that emerged in the cave asking me, "Who are you without Miranda?" As I wrote into my journal this question to which I had no answer, the pen ran out as I came to the letter *M* of my name. The invitation to hold on to nothing was loud and clear.

During this passage of fierce Grace, I found great sustenance sitting with an extraordinary female saint in India. Siva Sakthi Amma would give twice daily silent *darshan* (transmission) in silence, in a simple hall down a noisy side street in Tiruvannamalai, not far from Ramana Maharshi's ashram. Sitting with my eyes closed in meditation alongside up to forty others, I knew her serene presence had arrived into the room by the calm cool breeze beginning to pervade my consciousness. It let me settle deep into the still waters where nothing is ever rocked. These wordless meetings were so supportive in helping my nervous system begin adjusting to a significantly expanded, new reality for which I had no reference points and at the time could not claim to understand.

After three years of sitting with Siva Sakthi as often as I could on numerous trips to India, I was offered the opportunity of a private meeting. I had no idea what to expect. It was never my way to bow or prostrate at the feet of a guru, as I witnessed many westerners do. Something about that did not feel authentic. Yet the moment I was brought around the flimsy bamboo screen to stand before her petite form, wrapped in a faded orange sari, seated upon a cane chair, my body automatically dropped to the floor in full prostration. I wept and shook cathartically, completely awed by the blazing light and purity that was everything. "I" was nothing.

ESSENTIAL REGRET FOR HIDDEN ARROGANCE

My weeping was not emotion, not sadness, but inwardly I heard something inside saying "I'm sorry." It was not guilt, but a clean recognition of how blind I had been without even really knowing it. This essential regret that had me prostrating was so beautiful, and it naturally contained total forgiveness for my unconscious arrogant folly of thinking I had ever been the do-er, the owner of anything. In mystical openings since, I have come to see that we pass through a wave of cleansing regret for our ignorance each time we awaken into a new level of reality.

With a micro movement of one of Siva Sakthi's tiny fingers, my body sat bolt upright. Here, there was no personality, no story, no guru, just nakedly sitting with the true majesty that did not belong to anyone. In this angelic state of pristine purity way beyond "me" and "you," I understood why my heart had always been so moved by that final line in the Lord's prayer, "For thine is the kingdom, and the power, and the glory, forever and ever. Amen."

The depth of our heart can only be truly satisfied by the real—that is our Beloved, and there is no substitute. It is so heavenly whenever we are pierced open to perceive truly the way things are, beyond any filter of "me" or "my."

Perhaps you have had a glimpse of bowing to the mystery, when your newborn was placed into your arms for the very first time or when saying goodbye to a dying loved one whom you intuitively know you have spoken to for the last time. You are filled with an immense sense of privilege for the gift of all that has passed between you, including the disagreements. Perhaps you have felt humbled by the majesty of nature: the wild places that have not been manicured by any hand but God's. In the face of unarguable reality, your ego just settles back into its rightful place—the back seat of the car, beholding the majesty and gratefully enjoying the ride.

The following inquiry practice can help you journey through and beyond the stress and struggle of trying to lead yourself across the bridge from ego to essence. This series of questions can help melt your subtle pride, encourage you to empty out presumption, and soften into the receptive, not-knowing space. These questions can help you to just be here, be still, and hold on to nothing, kindly meeting everything that comes up along the way.

INQUIRY **Bowing to the Mystery**

You can journey into this sequence of questions as a meditation or put a timer on for ten minutes and journal your responses. I highly recommend doing them with a spiritual friend.

In what area of your life do you not know the way?
See what arises in your heart. Pay attention to the feelings that arise as the question moves through you. Remember there is no right or wrong response, so just be spontaneous and say whatever arrives without editing or feeling you have to rationalize. Let the next question take it further.

What's it like if you stay present, presume nothing, and allow not-knowing?
Let the question reverberate through your body, noticing the sensations, like heat, tension, energy, or tingling, and allow whatever comes to be named. Repeat these first two questions for at least ten minutes or more, noticing the insights, memories, feelings, and sensations that come. Whatever comes, remember there is nothing you have to fix or do. Just meet everything in the spirit of "thank you."

Now that you have exposed the blocks to humility, journey deeper with the following question for at least fifteen minutes. If working with a partner, loop back and forth with this one question.

What moves you to bow to the mystery?
Again, let the question reverberate through your body, heart, and mind, following the details of your own direct experience as it unfolds.

I defy anyone to stay with this question sincerely for any length of time and not begin to feel touched by the blessings of Grace—the felt sense of being given everything we truly need. When we come into intimate contact with the pure reality of existence, it is completely natural to bow, to happily settle back into the mystery and let it have its way with us. ~

Ultimately, humility not only melts our pride and breaks down the ignorance that makes us dense to receiving, it also gives us back to the naked truth of what we are. Humbly bowing to the mystery brings us into right relationship with the Source of our being, even if we have no formal name or prayer for that. Beautifully, it also brings us into right relationship with one another, with nature, with life itself. We become soft, peaceful, and fulfilled in the recognition that we are at the inner fountain—and always invited to take a deep drink of Grace.

7 PATIENCE

The Gentle Effort

I wearied myself searching for the Friend
with efforts beyond my strength.

I came to the door and saw how
powerfully the locks were bolted.

And the longing in me became that strong,
and then I saw that I was gazing
from within the presence.

With that waiting, and in giving up all trying,
only then did Lalla flow out
from where I knelt.

LALLA, *Naked Song* (translated by Coleman Barks)

So far in receiving the blessings of Grace, we have seen how trust reconnects us to the healing and holding of boundless love and how humility melts our subtle pride, opens inner space, and reconnects us to the exquisite purity that comes when we bow to the mystery. Patience helps us to greet the paradox of effort and effortlessness. Simultaneously it sharpens the lens of our practice, while relaxing the ego tendency to push. This is how the nourishing stream of Grace fills our inner cup with precisely what we need, in its own way and time.

The virtue of patience does not seem especially sexy on first glance. In our increasingly fast-paced, materialistic culture, we are used to ordering up whatever we want and receiving it with minimal wait time. Yet without strengthening the muscle of patience, we remain like spiritual children, insisting Grace deliver on our schedule. It is ironic that it takes such dedication to get out of the way and be as we are. Ego relaxation itself is a paradox. On one level, it is a state of Grace that provides a direct instantaneous vacation from the stress and struggle of your ego. At the same time, it is an advanced ongoing practice that calls for discrimination and devotion.

ALWAYS BEING, ALWAYS BECOMING

I once heard spiritual teacher Adyashanti share a lesser-known interpretation of the Buddhist heart sutra, *gate gate paragate, parasumgate, bodhi swaha*, as meaning "always being the Buddha, always becoming the Buddha." This expresses the true vision of nonduality that includes the Absolute and the relative levels of reality as part of one integrated stream.

On the Absolute level, there is no separation. You are always in and part of the Divine Being—meaning that all the Grace you could possibly need, all the love, peace, clarity, and joy is already yours. On this level your fears, concerns, and problems do not even exist, and nothing ever changes, even if you do not experience this as your emotional reality. Thus "be as you are" is an invitation to just accept the unchanging reality and recognize that you already rest in God. End of story.

Simultaneously, you and I manifest in time and form, like individual waves arising out of the one ocean. On the relative level, everything is constantly changing. Life is always presenting us with invitations to evolve through and beyond our veils: to grow physically, emotionally, and spiritually. Just as nature continues to cycle and unfold, there is no end to becoming more fully who we truly are.

So many people I meet in nonduality circles emphasize only the Absolute level, wanting to be past their "mom and dad" stuff. Yet there is a vast difference between conceptually knowing your true nature as that and truly living it. Until your mind is not referencing the past in any way; your heart is nonreactive, spontaneously loving to all beings; your body is relaxed, grounded, and settled; and you feel yourself abiding effortlessly and naturally at the inner fountain, given everything all the time, it is fair to say there is some becoming that wants to happen. As we have seen in previous chapters, so many of our ego patterns were laid down in childhood. Meditation teacher Loch Kelly articulates true awakening as a process of "waking up while growing up."[1]

EGO EFFORT VS. GENTLE EFFORT

Ramana Maharshi said, "There is a state beyond both effort and effortlessness: until it is realized, effort is required."[2] While it is ultimately Grace that brings back online the boundless love, clarity, peace, and joy of your true nature, it dances mysteriously with your gentle effort. This is a world away from your ego expending effort—from that pernicious tendency to push yourself into spiritual shape. Trying to push past your bad habits by grasping for some idealized state, rejecting how things are, creates a war inside that you cannot win.

Lao Tzu named this gentle effort, which brings us back into easeful flow, *wu wei*. To engage a steadfast dedication to be here, where you are, meeting all parts of your experience with a loving heart, doing nothing to rearrange it, is a simple but advanced practice. Great patience is needed because you cannot force ego relaxation any more than you can take the well-meaning advice of a friend telling you to "just relax" when you are really wound up. Likely, you feel like throttling them for being so irritating.

If you have been engaging in a spiritual practice for a while, you will know how frustrating it can be when despite your best efforts, your inner doors are tightly bolted. You are facing what needs to be faced, showing up on your meditation cushion, reading this book, and taking the time to do the inquiries and reflections. Still, here you go again, mind darting off into commentary, fear, judgment, anger. You cannot seem to stop manipulating in some subtle way, pushing and pulling for things to be other than what they are. You fear that if you don't push, nothing will change. Sometimes what we need most is to take our foot off the gas pedal.

PERSEVERE PATIENTLY, WITHOUT THE PUSH

In my early twenties I had the great blessing of studying meditation in a small Zendo in Oxford, England, where I was living at the time.

Fourteen of us would sit facing the wall in neat rows for two-hour stretches, broken up by some walking meditation and a koan that always made my head hurt. It was led by the formidable Sister Eileen MacInnes, a Catholic nun from Canada who served as a missionary in Japan. A truly interspiritual being, she was granted permission by her bishop to study Zen and ended up becoming a *roshi* (Zen priest).

The meditation practice began with traditional breath counting: count the breaths that come and go, and when distractions carry you away into thought, return to one. This was the preliminary concentration practice that led toward just sitting, just being. It took me six months to confess to Sister Eileen in a private interview that I never made it beyond the count of six! My impatient attitude regarded this as clear evidence of spiritual failure, and besides I was in a hurry to get past my many faults. However, Sister Eileen just kindly affirmed my effort and encouraged me to stay patiently with my practice. It took me years to appreciate the importance of her message.

In time, with patience and perseverance, my inner landscape began to refine. Although I could not point to when it happened, effortlessness emerged in my practice—I was not fighting off thoughts but letting them pass through without identifying with anything particular. The more I relaxed the race to get somewhere in particular in my meditation, the more nourishing and natural just sitting and being became. I started to look forward to formal practice, which I came to call my "morning gold." These eloquent words of Suzuki Roshi echoed my own experience: "The true practice of [meditation] is to sit as if you were drinking water when you are thirsty."[3]

Perhaps you already have some feel for the gentle effort through a hatha yoga class. Unless you have the body of a teenager, inevitably there are postures that are not so easy for you. To just avoid doing these difficult poses does not offer any growth in your practice. To just engage the poses you are already strong in can cause an imbalance. A wise teacher encourages you to move into the difficult postures, going as far as your body will allow, and then to stay there and breathe. Don't not do it, but don't force or push. Somehow, the body opens. Grace usually comes when you are not trying so hard. Still, you must do your part.

PRACTICE, BUT WITHOUT AN AGENDA

There are many contemporary teachers in the spiritual marketplace preaching a gospel that "no practice is necessary." Some hold the view that meditation, inquiry, and prayer keep us in the realm of becoming, seeking Grace in some future time. Read the biography of any spiritual giant, and you will be struck by their intense dedication, even after significant awakening. When Papaji (H. W. L. Poonja), the root guru of many popular nondual teachers, was asked whether he still practiced vigilance, he responded "until my last breath."[4] Ramana Maharshi spent fifteen years in silent meditation after realizing the unchanging Self and wrote countless *bhajans* (prayers) to his beloved Arunachala. The great Advaita sage Nisargadatta Maharaj did traditional Hindu*puja* (act of worship) several times a day, even though he taught, "I *am* that."

Most people find their way to spiritual practice motivated to resolve some struggle in their lives. There is nothing wrong with this because ultimately Grace does resolve the root of our struggle. It does so by inviting the source of the struggle (your ego) to retire as director of your life. Practicing, but without the agenda to arrive at some spiritual summit in the future, directly challenges any subtle bargaining that may be in the mix. It will flush out the subconscious trying to "buy" the blessings of Grace with spiritual good behavior.

The more you learn to softly surrender your demands and your subtle manipulation, the more the dense forces of your ego—the fear, control, and judgment—begin to melt. Yet having some awakening experiences does not mean that you are done with practice. Rather, your motivation for coming to prayer, meditation, and inquiry evolves. You explore your inner terrain not to get over some suffering but because you start to feel a natural love and devotion to whatever helps you marinate in the living waters.

FINDING YOUR WAY TO DRINK

Since Grace itself is effortless ease, patience helps us engage spiritual practices so we can flow harmoniously with what is. You do not need to chase after expanded states. Just be here, where you are, not pushing, not forcing yourself into some concept of enlightenment.

Engaging the gentle effort might take many forms. For you, it might be exploring which of the meditations, inquiries, and reflections in this book want to become part of the rhythm of your day. Perhaps it means setting aside a particular time and place in your house that you designate as sacred. Perhaps you already have years of formal practice under your belt. If this is the case, perhaps you might inquire into the question, "What would be most spiritually nourishing now?" If you have had a silent sitting practice, perhaps prayer is calling to be included. Perhaps it is chanting as you drive to and from work or cook dinner. Perhaps for you, journaling or walking in nature, staying present with every breath, is the gentle effort you need now. Remember the importance of humbly sitting in the unknown and not trying to find the answers. Rather, journey into the questions.

The blessings of Grace come when they come, with the insights, the synchronicity, the clarity, and the psychic nutrients we need. Yet just as praying hard for rain to come does not guarantee the end of drought, so Grace is mysterious. It needs the fertilizer of your sincerity, your willingness to show up and just be patient. Haiku poet Basho said it beautifully: "Sitting quietly, doing nothing, Spring comes, and the grass grows by itself." Let the following inquiry practice usher you beyond spiritual pushing.

INQUIRY **Beyond Spiritual Pushing**

Let these questions reverberate through your body, noticing your energetic and somatic experience and any feelings or insights that come. See if you can be specific, moving beyond one- or two-word answers to see more nuance, more detail, even if what comes does not make sense at first. Let all that bubbles up be greeted in the spirit of "thank you." Remember, you are not a problem to be fixed!

What limits you from engaging the gentle effort in your inner life?
Pay particular attention to any way you experience yourself pushing, perhaps trying too hard to get past some obstacle. Notice any chasing after special states. Notice any impatience, any frustration, or anything that prompts you to throw in the towel and not show

up for intimate soul time. Notice also if there is confusion about your practice or if you are mixing too many different approaches at once. Notice if any unworthiness is active or if there are hidden beliefs that taking time for the watering of your inner garden is somehow selfish. Notice if you are afraid of losing something or of the unfamiliar. Notice if you get off on being too busy.

What's it like, right now, if you just be here, curious and patient with this?
This question guides you to practice patience at your threshold. Perhaps insights come, revealing what practices, rhythms, and rituals want to be woven into the fabric of your day. A clue to this is feeling "I want to" rather than "I should" when contemplating a practice. If you listen, your true desire will help to ignite what Cabbalists call the "inner teacher"—the precise wisdom that can guide you into freedom and fulfillment. ~

OPENING TO DIVINE TRANSMISSION

The good news is that there is way more subtle support to help you relax, patiently engage the practices that call to you, and let the seas of your consciousness open than you typically recognize. When you are already giving your best and still you find yourself at a locked door, you can open up to a celestial helping hand.

Vedic cosmology asserts that our purity of motivation in our spiritual practice calls forth Vishnu—Divine Grace—who brings beneficent blessings to the sincere aspirant. Read any spiritual biography of a great being from the East or the West, and they often tell of direct encounters with celestial beings, angels, bodhisattvas, and awakened nonphysical beings. My dear friend Lama Palden Drolma, founder of the Sukhasiddi Foundation, explains this from within the nondual cosmology of Tibetan Buddhism: "Since all fully enlightened beings are beyond the boundaries of form and time, their blessings are available to us all the time, to support our practice, to nurture and sustain us in all our activities."[5]

This explains why many people have had such powerful direct encounters with a consciousness like Ramana Maharshi's, even half a century past his physical death. It's why many go on pilgrimage, whether to Assisi, Mecca, or Rumi's cave in Turkey, and receive some kind of transmission that brings an exquisitely attuned response to a deep need. You might pray to Tara or Christ in a challenging moment and somehow, things ease. The blessings of Grace often arrive when you are not looking—like in your dreams at night or in the passing smile of a stranger. It seems to know what you need better than you do.

You do not have to subscribe to a particular spiritual view to find yourself feeling a natural connection to an enlightened being or a particular embodiment of the Divine. Rarely do we get to choose this. Mysteriously, nonconceptual Grace usually finds its way to us. It can find you through reading a biography of a great master. A book or ancient text somehow might seem to emit a presence that you recognize but cannot logically explain. Perhaps just looking at the photograph of a sage or significant teacher plugs you in to a pristine consciousness way beyond any person or thing. Whatever it is that most moves your heart, do not dismiss it as mere fantasy. With gratitude, consciously lean toward it like a plant leans toward the light.

Ask this Grace to bless and guide your practice. Do not hold back from sincerely asking for anything you need help with in your life. Just do not make demands. Vedic scholar Sally Kempton writes, "When we ask an awake being to be present in our meditation, what we are actually asking is that this being's inner state of infinite clarity, luminous love and subtle awareness come alive in us."[6] You do not have to have "faith" in any particular religious view; although if you do, this can weave very naturally into this devotional aspect of practice.

GIVING UP TO NONCONCEPTUAL GRACE

There are many ways that we can begin opening to receive nonconceptual Grace, but sometimes we need to cut through our spiritual concepts first. Here is a simple way: Imagine you are hanging from a precarious branch at the edge of a steep ravine. There is no physical person around to help you. Recognizing this might be the end, who or what do you instinctively turn toward?

Mahatma Gandhi uttered the name "Ram" as he was slipping from this world to the next. You might feel a special connection to a particular embodiment of the Divine, such as Christ or Mary, Tara or Maitreya. Perhaps uttering the holy name "God," "Adonai," "Hu," or "Aum" brings an immediate feeling of the presence lighting up inside. It might be a mantra like Om Namah Shivaya or an ancient prayer like the Shema. It might be the name, face, or energy of your teacher that evokes the felt sense of blessings coming dynamically into the foreground of your experience. It does not matter so much what or who you call on; it matters more that you recognize that trying harder is not going to do it. Your job is to give up to a deeper Grace.

Sometimes, it is a line from a book or scripture that resounds through you like a plucked string. You can turn toward the consciousness that birthed this scripture into being and open to that. One of my formative spiritual teachers, Rabbi Joseph Gelberman, would always lovingly kiss his Torah before he opened it. Such devotion is essential for your inner life to blossom. It ends any interior dryness, making you feel spiritually fertile and juicy.

Remember how humility calls you to recognize that whatever you might understand or believe, the universe is way more mysterious than we can fathom. Just be open to possibilities beyond what you might have considered. See what happens as you engage in this meditation inviting you into the nonconceptual shower of Grace. I recommend that you engage in it daily at first. Once you have a feel for it, you can adapt it into a bedtime practice, as it is a very beautiful way to let go into restorative sleep. Enjoy!

MEDITATION **Resting in the Shower of Grace**

1. Create an altar in a quiet place where you will not be disturbed by placing before you one of the following: a picture of an awakened being or master teacher you feel a connection to or a book, sacred text, phrase, or mantra that evokes Grace beyond the mind.

2. Light a candle, and just gaze at your altar for a few minutes or as long as feels natural to you.

3. In your own way, place your forehead onto your expression of Divine Grace (your picture/book/mantra, etc.) as if bowing in love and gratitude. Open to blessings upon your practice and your life and dedicate whatever fruits come as blessings for all beings.

4. Sitting in an upright posture, close your eyes and turn within. Feel the natural rise and fall of your breath drawing you deeper in and down inside. Receive each inhale as a welcome and each exhale as a natural melting deeper into the present. Stay with this until you start to settle. If thoughts come, don't fight them; just don't follow them.

5. Inwardly, say the name of the Divine your heart loves best, the one you know is calling to you, or the mantra or short passage of sacred text (only a few words). Say this holy word or phrase with each exhale, first as a way to concentrate your awareness.

6. Stay with this holy word or phrase until you naturally start to feel your heart's love for that which this face or name or holy word calls forth in you. Stay with this devotion awhile.

7. See a hand of light upon your crown, as if that which you have called upon is dynamically here, transmitting into you their awakened consciousness of luminous love, limitless awareness, and every enlightened quality and beneficently blessing you with subtle nutrients and support.

8. Just as you naturally receive the light of the sun, which makes the daylight, see and sense yourself within a cosmic shower of scintillating golden light. You are already in it, and it contains the light of all enlightened beings, bodhisattvas, angels, and nonphysical dimensions of Grace. It also contains the love of anyone you have been close to who is no longer in physical form.

9. Marinate in this divine shower that contains every blessing. Feel the presence of that which knows you and loves you as eternally present. Be drenched in celestial blessings and completely restored.

10. Recognize that this presence represents all that is real and true about you and about everyone and everything. Feel yourself not only in the light but *part* of that light. You are claimed by it and given back to your true nature.

11. When you are ready, give thanks for all you have received.

12. Transition out of the formal meditation, and gently open your eyes, letting form and color come to you. Perhaps journal anything that comes. Repeat this practice often!

The more you deepen into your practice of ego relaxation—just being here, doing nothing, ceasing and desisting the subtle manipulation, yet sincerely showing up—the more Grace finds you. With patience, the parts of your consciousness that are still in a process of becoming settle down, like a boisterous pet settling peacefully into your lap. Somehow, if you are open, what it is that you most need finds you. Fresh understanding, wisdom, healing, gifts, and qualities come online, in their own time. ~

Just as scent is unseen by our physical eyes but has a powerful effect on our consciousness, the blessings of Grace are subtle but powerfully affect our life. The more you engage in the gentle effort, the more a divine hand comes, though you know not how. It can lift your life and practice to a whole new level. In time, and with patience, it is inevitable that one day you will open your eyes and see that you are gazing from within the presence itself. You begin to feel soft and full inside, naturally wanting to share the nectars with everyone.

8 ENTERING THE JOY OF BEING

All things are born out of bliss.
They live in bliss and dissolve into bliss.

TAITTIRIYA UPANISHAD

The more we settle into the practice of ego relaxation, the more Grace fills our inner cup with the nectars we need because Grace is boundless love, infinite generosity, and primordial bliss. It is both our unchanging ground and the blessings that mysteriously come from realms beyond conceptual understanding. Plato spoke of "the good" at the foundation of all things. It certainly requires deep trust, humility, and patience to stay intimate with this underlying goodness in a world so full of strife. Yet if we inquire into the cause of the painful displays of violence, greed, and hatred that blight our world, we see human beings caught in the spiritual poverty of lack, disconnected from the natural joy of being. We can end this unnecessary deprivation by slowing down, deepening into our heart, and relishing the gift of life.

Each year my husband and I take a three-week "do nothing" beach vacation, letting go of all our roles to simply be. Sitting cross-legged in meditation one day under the shade of our umbrella, I softly opened my eyes upon the endless blue sea and sky. The late afternoon light had turned golden, shimmering like diamonds on the water. I was in a deeply settled condition where the field of my awareness felt as vast as the horizon, dissolving the sense of inner and outer, when an enormous humpback whale leapt out of the sea, astonishingly close to the shore. Its massive form suspended in midair for a moment before pivoting and crashing down into the ocean with three playful slaps of its tail. Not only was this my first live whale sighting, but since I was so open from my meditation, it felt as if the whale was leaping out of my heart, ecstatically expressing the joy of being.

YOUR TRUE NATURE IS BEING-CONSCIOUSNESS-BLISS

Vedic philosophy views our true nature as *sat-chit-ananda*, "being-consciousness-bliss." What does this really mean? If there is one thing you could know for sure, it is that you exist. "Sat" is your beingness, your essence prior to your personality, the "I am" primordial purity that does not change and does not die. "Chit" is your consciousness, the witness of all your experiences. It gives rise to your awareness, not just to the contents of your experience but also to *knowing* yourself as awareness. "Ananda" is the nectar that pours forth from your deepest heart, a never-ending fountain of bliss, love, and joy.

Whenever you are deeply settled, conscious of what you are and what you abide within, ananda is your natural state. Since I was so open in that moment on the beach, the whale leaping out of the sea triggered me into ecstatic joy. I was awed by the power that made the whale want to propel his enormous body out of the ocean, just because he could. We want to be what we truly are, embodying and expressing our inherent qualities and unique gifts, just as a whale wants to leap out of the sea for the joy of it. Yet in our materialistic culture, authentic joy can feel elusive.

The World Health Organization cites depression as one of the greatest health crises in the Western world, despite the plethora of antidepressants and sophisticated therapeutic modalities at our disposal.[1] Our media preach a false gospel that joy is an object we can buy with more money and better things; that we earn it through becoming what we hope will buy the approval, love, or affirmation from others; and that we can achieve it through increasing our status. This external orientation keeps us seeking but never finding the real thing. It keeps us caught in ego concerns, disconnected from what is most natural.

YOUR HEART'S ESSENTIAL NATURE IS JOYFUL

Since ananda is the oceanic depth of your heart independent from personality, it is possible for love, joy, and even bliss to be present when things are going well and also when things feel like they are falling apart. The late Rabbi Joseph Gelberman, one of my early spiritual teachers and founder of the All Faiths Seminary, was the most joyful human being I have ever met. Narrowly escaping the rise of Nazism in his native Hungary, he secured safe passage to the United States but lost his wife, four-year-old daughter, seventeen brothers and sisters, and every other living relative to the gas chambers. I once asked him, "How are you so radiantly joyful when you have suffered such immense personal tragedy?" He took a breath, looked me in the eyes, and said softly, "I might not always be happy, but my soul's nature is joyful."

It is natural to prefer things to go your way, yet joy is not of the personality, nor is it circumstance dependent. Way more than just keeping a positive attitude, deeper than a wave of happiness, joy is the radiant tone of your deep heart itself. Since it is emerging from your pure being, which is timeless, changeless, and unshakable in its nature, it is possible, as Rabbi Gelberman discovered, to be joyful even when tremendous suffering is to be borne. The ticket price is feeling the full spectrum of your experience—the beauty and the horrors—and giving it all welcome in your heart.

Rabbi Gelberman befriended Swami Satchidananda, who initiated him into yoga and meditation to commune with his eternally joyful nature so he could grapple with his grief. He was very fond of chanting "*Adonai li v'lo ira*," Hebrew words taken from Psalm 23, meaning "The Lord is with me. I will not fear." He would visualize his family members in the gas chambers, singing and dancing and even praising, as their declaration that "the good" cannot be extinguished even in the face of the most grotesque human distortion. Rabbi Gelberman had extraordinary vitality into his nineties. His spirit of celebration and his gratitude for life never seemed far away.

LETTING THE MIND DROP INTO THE HEART

Abiding in our essential heart brings access to an intrinsic joy deeper than our emotional waves. The essential heart includes our ordinary emotions but gets very expansive and refined when it opens beyond the familiar sense of "you" and "I." When we stop clinging to thought or physical appearances and journey deeper into our felt interiority, we experience divine love and bliss *as* our heart. It can feel as if the back of your heart is a portal to galaxies of Grace, out of which the beautiful qualities of empathy, kindness, compassion, beauty, courage, and joy emerge exponentially.

In a nondual state of boundless love, you not only feel that loving goodness pervading all things, you also recognize that you *are* this love. The more this opens, the more you recognize there is nothing outside of this love, this goodness—not even cancer. Our mind can only understand how this is possible once it has surrendered dominion and lets the heart itself lead. This is why Ramana Maharshi kept reminding his devotees to let the mind drop into the heart. It is through deepening in the heart that we feel the qualities we need to greet the inevitable complexities of life. This itself is cause for joy. It eradicates the root of depression by deeply connecting each of us to all that is truly meaningful.

Ego relaxation, while deceptively simple, has the power to refine, uplift, and significantly expand your consciousness. Grounding in the present moment and opening to sense, feel, and allow everything without collapsing, rejecting, or rearranging, you are returned to deeper reality. Joy blossoms as you recognize you are already at home, even though you might have been dreaming of exile. *A Course in Miracles* points out, "You are truly happy only when you know you abide in God. That is the only environment in which you will not experience strain, because that is where you belong."[2]

JOY IS NOT EARNED OR DESERVED

Almost everyone has received impressions from parents, culture, or religion that "the good" is something that needs to be earned by some form of good behavior. All parents need to train their young in what is workable and unworkable behavior through some form of reward and punishment (hopefully not too harsh). Perhaps you were allowed to do something enjoyable as a "reward" for being good or given a "treat" for completing your homework, for example. Perhaps something you enjoyed was withheld as a form of punishment, like being grounded if you stepped out of line.

If you have had a strong religious upbringing, you may have been given the impression that you were unworthy of joy. This can lead to a pervading sense of guilt about pleasure, that somehow it is not morally right to be expansive and joyous when others are suffering.

No one in their right mind would hold a baby in their arms and say it does not deserve joy and love because it has not yet proved itself or earned it. Likewise, no one would feel that a baby should not be allowed to laugh because someone else in the family is grieving. Similarly, you do not have to be obedient to the impressions you absorbed. You can change the channel just as you would turn the dial away from the static noise of a bad radio station.

WHAT LIMITS YOUR ACCESS TO ANANDA?

Just as a hard chunk of ice melts back into its original state of water when met by the warmth of the sun, unconditionally allowing the totality of your experience in the present moment melts the blocks to ananda.

Surely the greatest inhibitor of joy is taking the nagging, judgmental voice of your superego seriously. It can return to sit on the throne of your consciousness, posing as your "conscience," jabbing at you with fearful caution against letting go into joy. Remember that your superego evolved to help your basic ego structure function, but now your focus is ego relaxation. A mature seeker once shared with me that when she catches a hint of superego judgment squashing the naturally expansive energy of joy, she takes a breath and tells her inner critic, "Go to Tahiti and get laid." A playful approach can be a great ally in intercepting the cycle of negative inner commentary, and besides, it is a joyful way to kick that imposter off the throne.

Another significant inhibitor to ananda is the concern that you might expand so much that you lose control. Perhaps you fear losing your capacity to function appropriately in the world, thereby saying and doing things that cause havoc in your relationships. At the core of our concerns with ananda is usually the fear that if our instinctual drive for pleasure took over we would just run amuck, indulging ourselves without any kind of brake.

One of the hallmarks of addiction, whether to food, alcohol, drugs, sex, gambling, or spending, is that the addict is not truly enjoying their present experience. While they are turning to activities that light up pleasure centers in the brain, their indulgence is an extreme form of rejection, grasping, and self-abandonment. The suffering of indulgence is driven by disconnection from the deep heart and its joy. This usually feels like an agitated, anxious inner state of deprivation. This compels an addict to seek a quick fix to get away from that state. However, it fails to satisfy because anything we use to escape some feeling or chase after a particular kind of high leads us further away from our heart.

If you have a history with addiction, I recommend rereading the earlier chapters on fear and trust and exploring what limits your capacity to *trust your true nature*. Then, find someone skilled and safe to help you get to the core of what holds this all together. Most of all, engage the patient, gentle effort in taking back your basic human right to be free from the false god of addiction.

BEWARE OF CHASING AFTER EXPANDED STATES

So often we substitute the chasing after love and joy externally with the spiritual materialism of chasing after high spiritual states. One of the most common questions I am asked about meditation, usually soon after giving a new practice, is, "Why am I not experiencing bliss yet?"

Ananda is not something we can chase. It comes when we patiently open to what is naturally miraculous in the here and now of each moment. This means we do not have to obtain anything different than what we already have. Settling into the simplicity of our direct, ordinary experience and relaxing the chase for anything particular ushers us into the receptive state. Sometimes the blessings of Grace bring forth a quiet contentment and sometimes an ecstatic state. When ananda flows, there is no chasing—just naturalness, spontaneity, and freedom.

DISCRIMINATING THE TRIGGER FROM THE CAUSE

We often confuse the arising of ananda with that which triggered it. For example, your joy might be triggered by the delight of playing with your grandchild, the sensual bliss of intimacy with your lover, or the warm companionship of a dear friend. Perhaps what pops your heart most is drinking in the scent of a blossoming rose, listening to some fabulous music, ecstatically letting go to the beat on the dance floor, feasting on art and beauty, or the rush of being at a sporting event. So many things can trigger deep joy within us, but the location of this joy itself is your own heart.

When you contact ananda directly, it can feel like rich golden nectar is expanding throughout your consciousness, rippling waves of pleasure in the body and dissolving boundaries of the mind. Ananda supports ego dissolving by melting our sense of separation into the ocean of bliss. The more you discriminate the triggers from the cause of your joy, the more you recognize the inherent joy of your being. You start feeling that your heart is an ocean of ananda. So many little things can activate you into experiencing the joy of life. This makes you less dependent on particular conditions and people to experience it. You become softer and more content.

The key is not getting too attached to the triggers of your ananda, for all things in this world change. Grandchildren can become moody teenagers, intimate relationships go through their ups and downs, our bodies age, and our faculties can diminish. To become attached to one form that opens your heart is to miss the point.

CELEBRATING THE GIFT OF YOUR LIFE

The more you recognize that you did not birth yourself into existence, the more it becomes clear that you do not own this life. It is a gift, and it is to be enjoyed. The third-century Rabbi Arika shared the Talmudic perspective: "We will have to account to God for all the good things our eyes beheld but which we refused to enjoy."[3] *The Radiance Sutras*, a Tantric text translated by Lorin Roche, expresses it beautifully:

Tasting dark chocolate,
A ripe apricot,
A luscious elixir—
Savor the expanding joy in your body.
Nature is offering herself to you.
How astonishing
To realize this world can taste so good.

When sipping some ambrosia,
Raise your glass,
Close your eyes,
Toast the universe.
The Sun and the Moon and the Earth
Danced together
To bring you this delight.
Receive the nectar on your tongue
As a kiss of the divine.[4]

In recent years I have learned to ski. In the winter, I love to fly down a mountain in Lake Tahoe, aptly called Heavenly. My husband and I ski side by side with coordinated iPods listening to the same music. Neither of us can contain the enormous smile on our face as we whiz down to views of pristine waters surrounded by majestic snowcapped mountains. It is ecstatically joyful, pleasurable. I am intensely awake to the sacred gift of life and unabashedly enjoying it here and now.

Consciously celebrating the blessings of life is part of an integrated spiritual practice. It is how we acknowledge the gifts of our life and gratefully receive them. We naturally feel thankful that our good fortune is not earned or deserved—but is given. It is a dynamic form of bowing to the mystery, in praise.

The next time you are triggered into a state of joy—perhaps getting down to some fabulous music on the dance floor, eating your favorite treat, leisurely cooking a meal for loved ones, arranging flowers in your home, or taking in the way the light pours through the trees on a walk—drink in the moment as a form of worship. Ego relaxation is not just about helping you deal with challenges, it invites you to deepen into your bliss as well. This following inquiry shows you how. Go deep and have fun with this!

INQUIRY **Entering into Ananda**

Take some breaths, feeling yourself welcomed into the present moment exactly as you are. Sense your body and inner atmosphere, allowing it to be. Inquire into these questions, sequentially, starting with the first question and letting the subsequent questions invite you to journey further.

What triggers your heart to soar in joy?
See what comes, name it, and then let the following question take things further.

What causes this to arise?
Explore where the delight comes from that is deeper than its trigger. Let yourself feel into whatever you can of the cause. Do not think about it too much, as your ordinary, linear mind cannot lead here, so drop out of it and let your heart lead. Notice what happens in your body as well.

What's it like if you enter into the cause of this joy?
How does it feel if you surrender into where this joyful experience is coming from, without reservation? What is it like energetically in your body? What feelings arise within your heart? How might this help you simply acknowledge and receive the blessings of Grace?

The thinking mind cannot lead us into such an inquiry, but we can let our consciousness lean into wherever the questions take us. There is no wrong or right answer, just an invitation to let the heart lead us back into intimacy with itself. Notice how this affects your consciousness: you will likely feel abundant and generous, and your joy and fulfillment will likely act as sunshine for others. ~

RADIANT JOY BEYOND SELF-CENTEREDNESS

Contemporary spiritual master A. H. Almaas used the Sufi term *ridhwan* for the mystical school that he founded. It means "a soul that is satisfied." Feeling settled and satisfied is evidence that you are growing more present, learning to trust, being humble in the face of the mystery, and being with the paradoxes of life patiently. Natural happiness comes online as you recognize and receive the blessings of Grace.

The more contact you have with your true heart, the more the sense of lack and deprivation disappears. You start to perceive and feel your own good fortune. Your heart takes on abundant fullness, a natural gratitude that radiates outward. Not only does this make life so much sweeter, it also makes you less narcissistic. Since true joy expands your heart beyond "yours" and "mine," you naturally feel your interconnectedness with everything and everyone. This manifests into a virtue Buddhists call "sympathetic joy"—a sense of joy at the good fortune of others.

You begin to enjoy the diversity in our world, taking pleasure in the unique expression of others, delighting in the divine play. Feeling your connection to the Source of all satisfaction powerfully frees up your life-force energy. It feels like having a fountain of nectar circulating and radiating within your heart.

The more you let the triggers call you deeper into the cause of ananda that is your own heart, the more joy becomes not just a state but also an inner platform. I notice that I often wake in the morning with a sense of excitement, curious about what words, chant, line of inquiry, or meditation process I could share to help others get a taste of the Grace I feel so fortunate to have stumbled upon. This is a revolutionary turnaround considering my historical struggles with clinical depression.

I notice that it takes way less stimulus to be joyful than it used to. I find deep pleasure in everyday things: Seeing a baby lizard scurrying behind some rock on a morning walk feels so delightful. The springtime explosion of pink blossoms as I drive to and from my errands feels orgasmic. Just seeing my husband's face when he walks through the door at the end of the day brings a wave of warm appreciation through my body.

I feel the essence of Psalm 23's conclusion, penned so many years ago, that has brought so many beings back to remembering the blessings of Grace, living from the awareness that you and I are being given everything, always.

> You anoint my head with oil;
> my cup overflows.
> Surely goodness and mercy shall follow me
> all the days of my life,
> and I shall dwell in the house of the Lord
> forever.[5]

Ultimately, gratitude is not something you "do" as a strategy to feel happy. Rather, its arising is evidence that you are aware of the blessings of Grace and are in the receptive state. The following meditation shows you how to simply receive and radiate the Grace you are discovering.

MEDITATION **Receiving and Radiating Grace**

This is a simple practice that you can weave into your everyday life. It does not require any special posture or time frame. You can simply use it to turn moments in your life into a powerful meditation practice. Here's how: Whenever you are aware of being given any kind of gift or feeling any evidence of "the good," take a deep breath as if drinking in this Grace through your entire being. Drink in the goodness as if letting it penetrate your body, going right into the marrow of your bones. Let it touch your heart and recognize that this gift is the mystery saying, "I love you; here, have this." Let it awaken your mind as if drinking light and nourishment.

With your exhale, feel this goodness radiating toward everyone: toward those you know, those you bump into but do not know personally, and everyone everywhere who might be in need of spiritual nectar in some way. You can learn to live your life from the naturalness of this meditation, incorporating it into a walking meditation or while lying in bed curled up with your beloved spouse or even your pet. Practice this any moment that you are triggered into recognizing that you are blessed. ~

Cultivating trust, bowing in humility, practicing the gentle effort, and entering the joy of being have a nourishing effect on your consciousness. You might notice that you are beginning to feel spiritually hydrated, as if a spring is bubbling up from within, and perhaps also that you truly are in a refined shower of subtle light, raining down from realms your mind might never fully understand. You grow stronger and happier and more open. This provides a powerful platform to dive into a whole new dimension of Grace . . . and it wants to take you somewhere new.

PART III

THE TRANSFORMING POWER OF GRACE

Drink my wine and you will become me.
And all that is hidden you will see
With your own eyes.

GOSPEL OF THOMAS

Grace is the living presence that is not only the cause of your being and not just the blessings that fill your heart. Grace is the mystical power that lifts your veils, transforming you to higher consciousness.

Each dimension of Grace has a particular way of resolving your struggle by reconnecting you to the boundless qualities of your true nature. The ground of Grace feels like being part of a mountainous presence that supports you to be present and relax out of defensive fear, control, and judgment. The blessings of Grace awaken the sense of being cared for, showered with gifts and subtle nectars that fill your inner cup and end the spiritual drought.

Yet Grace does not stop at placating your troubles; it wants to dissolve your barriers and bring you all the way home into the full embodiment of who you really are. As you deepen into the practice of ego relaxation, Grace goes to work on you, flushing out to the light of awareness whatever might be limiting your full freedom.

Imagine that you are hiking in a remote, mountainous area and you happen upon a magnificent waterfall—not a little stream, but a dynamic unfolding body of water. It tumbles over craggy rocks, somehow flowing and falling gracefully around rugged terrain. The waterfall does not struggle or push but uses the momentum of gravity to slide over the boulders, naturally yielding to flow with the least resistance. It pours into a vast expanse, bridging one platform of earth to another. In the process of its unfolding, everything the living water touches is transformed, either by becoming green and verdant or by being dissolved.

Whenever we happen upon a waterfall, we feel the activity of the transforming power of Grace. We are naturally humbled and moved by the undeniable intelligence, power, and majesty. The living water draws us to dip our feet or cup our hands in it, or perhaps even to strip off our clothes and get in. Intuitively, we know it is miraculous.

In Christian and Sufi mystical literature, "wine" is code for "living water," the alchemical spiritual substance that transforms our consciousness to realms beyond the ordinary. Jesus's first "miracle" is the turning of water into wine at the wedding at Cana. Reflecting on this parable afresh, nowhere does it mention who is getting married. Perhaps it is not really an outer marriage of people, but a mystical inner marriage: the dissolving of inner masculine and inner feminine, the marriage of dual and nondual, inner and outer, physical and nonphysical, ego and essence. The transforming power of Grace not only sets us free from unnecessary polarity, it also wants to take us somewhere new if we will surrender to it.

Most importantly, the transforming power of Grace helps us deal with the tough terrain that every human life involves: the betrayals, the hurts that are hard to bounce back from, the places where we get stuck in deeply entrenched patterns. We need Grace to help us address these challenges of being human.

The next four chapters are an invitation to come to the waterfall. Dive in through time-tested spiritual technologies of forgiveness, true compassion, unwinding ego identity, and abiding in your boundless nature. Ultimately, you cannot *do* spiritual transformation. As you yield to the transforming power of Grace, it finds you.

9 FORGIVENESS

Transforming Heartbreak

A piercing word.
A stab of betrayal.
The boundary crossed.
A trust broken.
In this lacerating moment,
Pain is all you know.
Life is tattooing scripture into your flesh,
Scribing incandescence in your nerves.
Right here,
In this single searing point
Of intolerable concentration,
Wound becomes portal.
Brokenness surrenders to
Crystalline brilliance of Being.

LORIN ROCHE, ***The Radiance Sutras***

Recognizing that we abide within and are part of the deepest Grace imaginable is truly a cause for joy, but it does not mean we can skirt around the grit of being human. Getting close to anyone who is not fully enlightened inevitably brings the risk of some shrapnel lodging itself in our tender heart. Any unconscious conflicts that have not been resolved inside will inevitably seep out in difficult ways for others. The Grace of forgiveness helps us harness our relational hurts so we can shift into a whole other dimension of consciousness.

All wisdom traditions agree that forgiveness is crucial for bringing us back into right relationship with ourselves and one another. Forgiveness restores inner peace by cleansing our minds of blame. It heals the wounds of the heart—both those we have given and those we have received. Most importantly, forgiveness helps us deal with the taboo emotions of rage, envy, and hatred that few of us want to admit to, yet tumble out of us when we are caught in some untenable pain. Given the destruction born of unresolved grievances in our world, we need the medicine of true forgiveness now more than ever.

Try as you might, you cannot force forgiveness. I was eighteen years old when a friend persuaded me to take the Forum, the latest version of Werner Erhard's infamous Erhard Seminars Training. I was the youngest of sixty people locked in a room for two weekends, listening to a trainer confronting us on our "bullshit." This macho approach to transformation was so energetically jarring I struggled to stay awake. However, I do remember the insistence that to attain inner freedom, you had to forgive your parents.

I could barely stay in my body when an overzealous assistant handed me the telephone, pressuring me then and there to tell my mother and father that I loved them. I wiggled out of it with some excuse but agreed to call home and communicate my forgiveness before the next weekend. Two days later, I totaled my already beat-up car in a head-on collision. Unconsciously, I would rather kill myself than enter what felt like an impossible conversation with the two people who had given me life. At that time, I had many complex feelings that I had no idea how to address. I learned at a young age that there is way more to forgiveness than glossing over a hurt and playing nice.

BEWARE OF PHONY FORGIVENESS

Forgiveness is a powerfully transformative spiritual technology, but it is wildly misunderstood. Consider how you feel when someone shares their judgment of something you said or did, presumes their perception is objective, and then says, "I forgive you." You would not be alone if such a declaration trigged intense irritation. When you hold a grievance and then take the spiritually noble position of "rising above it," not only is it nauseating, it is not forgiveness.

Neither is forgiveness righting a wrong. Liberation does not come by insisting another admit their "sin," agreeing with your condemnation of them as "guilty" and submitting to some "penance" for their error. The late theological scholar Kenneth Wapnick called this vicious circle of sin-guilt-punishment the "unholy trinity of the ego." Sadly, this punitive consciousness pervades our world's justice system. Allegiance to this kind of thinking keeps us all enslaved in ego, the result of which is succinctly explained in the familiar aphorism often attributed to Mahatma Gandhi: "An eye for an eye makes the whole world blind."

We tend to confuse forgiveness with ego attempts at reconciliation—trying to get another to understand our position, accept our view, and agree to change. I have often wondered whether our collective attempts at reconciliation and social justice might be more successful if we walked through the gate of true forgiveness first.

TRULY TURNING THE OTHER CHEEK

The liberating breeze of forgiveness comes mysteriously by Grace, and it calls for a particular kind of surrender. It challenges us to "turn the other cheek," which understood from a mystical lens is not being a martyr and letting an aggressor sock it to you once more; it is a turning away from the external orientation of ego that seeks to correct errors "out there" and instead taking the log out of your own eye first.

Forgiveness means tilling the soil of your own consciousness more thoroughly. It will ask you to question your perceptions of who did what and why, suspending all projection of guilt and blame. It will ask you to let go of all positions. Most of all, it will call you to surrender everything that feels so impossible on the inner altar of the unified heart. You cannot "do" forgiveness. Essentially, it calls for a shift out of identifying with ego altogether—yours or another's.

Forgiveness begins when you want true peace more than you want to be right, to be in control, or to hold the moral high ground. While choosing peace sounds simple enough, consider the last argument you had with a family member or spouse, and you might recognize how hard it can be to let go of the insistence that "if you change, I can be at peace." Yet true forgiveness does not ask you to pour pink paint over a cracked wall.

FORGIVENESS IS A PROCESS

In my first book, *Boundless Love,* I wrote about the stages of forgiveness gleaned from working through a difficult dynamic with my father. It took great dedication to turn more substantially within and address my grievances. First, I had to harness all my strength to cease feeding any story of blame. Then, I had to stay present in my body and honestly meet the hurt and rage lodged deep in my cells, while sincerely wanting to find another way. This meant contacting the forces that kept me bound in such unworthiness, not bypassing the traumatic history with some spiritual platitude.

Practicing ego relaxation with it all, I discovered there was a living presence independent of my personality that I could lean into with this complex web of suffering. At this inner altar, the holy of holies within the heart, I could take down my defensive armor. I could also admit the hurts I had dished out in the mix. Only then could I engage the heart of true forgiveness, which was to join with my father, not from my ego to his, but essence to essence. I landed in the inviolable truth of ever-present love that embraces us all.

The day I was able to genuinely see my father minus the thick lens of blame was an inner revolution. My distorted projection gave way to clear undivided vision. It brought peace to my mind and a new depth to my heart but also a sweet acceptance of my father without the need for a hashing out of the history. The cleansing Grace of forgiveness brought not only love but also discriminating wisdom in how to navigate the differences in our relating more skillfully.

Forgiveness requires you to let go of trying to sort out any ruptures ego to ego. Instead, you come to the unified ground of your consciousness, where you are restored to a love that is not just fluffy and sweet—it is objective vision. It comes by Grace, and it resolves conflict at the root.

THE FORGIVENESS PARADOX

Forgiveness contains a curious paradox: that we are innocent in eternity but not in time. Thus to engage this transforming Grace, we need to approach it from an integrated nondual perspective.

As we have seen, our true nature is not only changeless infinite consciousness, it is pristine, stainless, *indestructible innocence.* Who we truly are remains untarnished by any mistake and can never be violated. This is good news for us all, for it means we can thrive even after unspeakable injustice and cruelty.

However, on the relative level, even when it is not our intention to stumble in ignorance, it happens all too easily. Mature spiritual practice requires that we acknowledge not just our good intentions but also our difficult impact on one another. At the same time, remember that none of us is defined by our mistakes.

I do not believe that it is a matter of asking God for forgiveness, since there is no condemnation possible in the mind of infinite love and unity. However, given the pain we tend to cause one another and the ways we so often hurt ourselves, we need Grace to help us forgive our common humanity. Since at the deepest level we are not separate but individual waves arising out of the one sea of consciousness, to forgive another *is* to forgive yourself.

ADDRESSING THE FEARS OF FORGIVENESS

We all long for liberation, but forgiveness can feel so outrageous in the face of the tough terrain we all traverse at times: a rupturing divorce, a betrayal of a best friend, a crushing conflict with our parent or child. Whenever we perceive ourselves to be unfairly treated, it can feel like an impossible task to join in that deeper ground where we are not our mistakes.

When caught in deep hurt, our ego will counsel that forgiveness is just not smart. Perhaps you fear that forgiveness will make you into a passive doormat, allowing no protection for your vulnerable heart. Perhaps you fear that forgiveness means you cannot say no when something does not feel respectful, either for yourself or for another.

Susan, a dedicated student who had a painfully explosive history with her sister, shared her fear: "If I question my perception of who she is, that means I have to question *all* of my perceptions, all that I have presumed to be real, including my sense of who I am." Forgiveness can feel very edgy to our familiar identity, which wants to receive transforming Grace while maintaining the status quo.

Perhaps you fear that forgiveness condones injustice, believing that hard-hearted condemnation is necessary to hold a boundary on workable behavior. There are times when it may be wise to step back from a situation that has become too emotionally charged to be healthy. However, there is a vast difference between taking time out to cool down so you can inquire into the roots of your own reactivity and icing someone out of your heart.

Whenever you condemn another, write them off, or annihilate them with your mind, you are caught in the grip of hatred. It is for this reason that forgiveness is the great need of our world.

UNDERSTANDING OUR TABOO EMOTIONS

Hatred, rage, and envy are not pretty, but they are part of the human condition. Since the pernicious problems on our planet revolve around some untenable heartbreak that turns to hard hatred, explodes in rage, or festers in envy, we must understand these shadow features of our humanity, which need our forgiveness rather than our condemnation.

If you are a parent, I am sure you have heard your children say, "I hate you, Mommy (or Daddy)" when you will not allow them to do something they want. A. H. Almaas has an important perspective on the root of these taboo emotions. In essence, he says that hatred is our ego's reaction to an untenable heartbreak and feeling oppressed and powerless in our situation. I am sure you know all too well the searing pain when another's behavior feels too violating to bear. It can feel like the only solution is to cut yourself off, harden your heart, or strike back in revenge. Energetically in our body, hatred feels icy, cold, and hard, like we don't care. While hate is our ego's attempt to deal with an untenable hurt, cutting anyone out of your heart will disconnect you from *your* loving heart. We see this in the *heartless* behavior of so many tyrants on our world stage. Terrorism, for example, is a palpable symbol of the ego's attempt to offset heartbreak through revenge. Hatred is a distortion of our true essential power.

Rage is an instinctive reaction to feeling disrespected, mistreated, or neglected. The turn of phrase, "He made my blood boil," expresses how hot, fiery, and explosive rage feels. Perhaps you recall a moment when another's actions felt so outrageous and so violating that you had to "go big" energetically, attempting to push the seeming source of the offense out or attack back to let them know how much they have hurt you. Again, rage is not wrong, but it is a distortion of our true strength, which guides us to instead clearly but calmly draw a boundary, speak up, or take a different action where necessary.

Envy is a reaction to our ego's felt sense of impoverishment. It emerges when we feel deprived of something we so want but believe we have no access to. Perhaps you have found yourself fixating on someone who has what you desire—be it a wonderful new relationship, good fortune with finances or their career, or the ability to easefully express a luminous gift. When we are "green with envy," it usually feels very shameful. Secretly hating another for daring to have what we believe we cannot is the root cause of theft, rampant materialism, and unhealthy competition.

Acting upon any form of hatred, rage, or envy will destroy any possibility of inner peace because our true nature is not separate: to attack another, even with your mind, is to attack yourself. Yet it can be hard—when you feel so mistreated or slighted, and things feel so unfair—not to give in to the dark side.

UNWINDING PROJECTION AND SPLITTING

Forgiveness unwinds our projections, and specifically, our perception that someone is guilty and needs to be punished. Forgiveness asks us to suspend trying to spiritually police the universe for a moment and instead focus on addressing our inner violence, which we often deny exists or else project onto some "other."

True forgiveness brings its heavenly breeze down to earth and into our human hearts by unwinding what the late Scottish psychiatrist Dr. Ronald Fairbairn coined the "splitting of the ego." This mechanism gets laid down in early childhood, when we do not yet have the capacity to understand how the same person (our mother or father) can contain many different qualities, some beautiful and some difficult. Internally, we learn to separate out the "bad" unfulfilling aspects to protect the "good" satisfying parts of our primary caregivers. We project this splitting mechanism onto everything and everyone—rejecting the bad in others and in ourselves to protect the good. This is how duality starts to feel normal.

While this might sound abstract, recall the last argument you had with your spouse or someone you truly love. It is humbling to find how deeply entrenched we can get in the belief that our position is the good one, the right one. Most writings on forgiveness focus on getting past the sense of being violated in some way by another. Reflecting on the most challenging heartbreaks of my own life, the nucleus of the transformation has always involved taking back my projection of the other as "all bad" and forgiving myself for the undigested divisions within my own consciousness.

We do not need to look far to see how destructive justifying our position as "all good" can be. All wars start from projecting the bad out there and then justifying the need for revenge. We need Grace to restore our split minds, heal our hearts, and show us another way. Forgiveness calls us to surrender—not to another's ego but to a deeper truth.

TRUE CORRECTION OF ERROR

It's obvious that we all need a course correction from time to time. Yet our ego cannot be in charge of the process. Atonement happens entirely through love, in a chamber of our heart that has no owner.

The word *atonement*, truly understood, captures the very essence of forgiveness. It is a purification that corrects our distortion at the root and at the same time brings us into "at-one-ment," the unified condition. Forgiveness thus bridges the relative and the absolute levels of our being, lifting us to a whole new ground where we gain liberation and objective clarity. This gives us true discrimination to see through the eyes of love, while simultaneously recognizing where someone is in their consciousness and acting appropriately given the situation.

Yet guilt, blame, and the need for any kind of punishment or revenge are completely removed. Since the word *sin* literally means "missed the mark," there need not be any heavy condemnation to seeing our own distortions and receiving correction. Only we must remember that it is not our role to lead the correction. Grace is the purifier.

THE HEART-CAVE OF ABSOLUTE LOVE

True forgiveness happens in what Ramana Maharshi called the "interior of the heart-cave, where the one reality shines as I-I."[1] If you do not limit your heart to merely being the seat of emotions but journey deeper and further back into the cavity in your chest, at some point you will begin to feel a vast, loving space that has no beginning or end. It can feel as if your heart opens to the infinite galaxy. Some report experiencing it as being within an infinite field of dark velvety presence or pervaded by luminous light. While the way it comes alive for each of us is very personal, we recognize this as the holy of holies—the inner sanctuary deeper than "your" heart or "mine." Here, we breathe the clean air of our shared identity, the affect of which is Absolute Love.

This depth of heart will melt the fundamental activity of your ego to split the good and the bad, for all angels and all demons are welcome to come home. Here, all projections can unwind. You naturally start recognizing that whatever you do, you do to yourself. You see the distortion of your own ego and recognize that *you* are not the corrector; Grace is.

In this depth of the heart, you can surrender all that you do not know how to resolve—be that a conflict with your sister or spouse, outrage at a collective group of people, or some grievance you hold about yourself—on the nonconceptual altar of Absolute Love. Forgiveness invites us not to bypass but rather to bring the complexity of our humanity to an inner altar. Here, the eyes of the heart open to an undivided vision, where the distortions of good and bad are miraculously cleansed, and we are returned to love.

The following exercise is a powerful practice that blends reflective inquiry with a meditation designed to open you to the Grace of forgiveness.

INQUIRY AND MEDITATION

The Grace of Forgiveness

There are two ways you can engage in this practice. The first is to practice it when you find yourself getting caught in anger, resentment, or envy. Anytime you become aware of an irritation with someone, including yourself, it is a sign that a grievance is active in your consciousness, and thus doing this practice for a handful of days in a row will be extremely beneficial.

Alternately, you could work with this practice once a week, as a way to "clean house," continuing to bring any shadow material into the light. Trust your intuition as to what feels best for you.

Since true forgiveness requires you to honestly meet your grievances—the hurts that keep you looping back into a pattern of conflict—it is important that you do not push past the hurt. Rather, just name it without commentating on whether or not it should be there. Also it is especially important that you stay connected with the sensations and energy in your body, as this particular terrain of your grievances is likely to bring up the suppressed energy of anger, hurt, and hate. This might feel like a fiery heat or icy coldness flashing through your body, or parts may feel cut off. Just name this and feel it in the spirit of ego relaxation.

1. Sit in a sacred space, where you will not be disturbed, with your journal or a friend.

2. For ten minutes or more, explore the following question: *What grievance do you wish to place on the altar of the heart-cave?* (Consider hurts you have given and the ones you have received, including those that feel "minor" as they are equally disruptive to your peace of mind.)

3. Close your eyes, turning your attention within for the meditation. Bring your awareness to the breath, letting each inhale and exhale guide you to melt in and down.

4. Bring your awareness to the heart. With each inhale, feel your desire for true peace and liberation in this process, yet without concern about how to get there. Just breathe into your heart and cultivate your true desire. Stay with this awhile.

5. Feel yourself being drawn to the back of the heart, to a place that is deep, dark, and quiet. It might feel as if your heart backs onto the infinite galaxy, but be open to however the heart-cave shows itself to you. Here you find an empty altar that welcomes everything without exception. Above the altar is a spotlight.

6. In your own way, lay on the altar your grievances, the impossible conflicts, and the hurts you do not know how to get past or forgive, asking for liberating Grace to restore you to the truth behind all appearances.

7. Lay down your judgments, anything you have rejected as "bad."

8. Lay your most significant relationships on this inner altar.

9. Lay whatever you find heartbreaking in our world on this inner altar.

10. Lay yourself down on the altar. Ask to be cleansed of all error, all misperception, all distortion.

11. See, feel, or sense a transparent, cleansing aqua mist pervading everything and everyone that has been placed on the altar. It might feel like soft healing vapor. Let this presence of forgiveness cleanse all errors at the Source, unwind distortion, and remove all veils. It restores everyone to indestructible innocence and complete unity, our original pristine condition.

12. Be open to any additional insight that comes, and then when you are ready, return to the inquiry with the following question for ten minutes or more: *What's it like in the heart-cave of Absolute Love?* ~

In the depth of the heart, all duality falls away. All distortion falls away. The need to reject anything falls away. Giving up your position and your attachment to what you thought would bring correction allows the Grace of forgiveness to arrive. All errors are corrected by the ultimate purifier. The slate is wiped clean. Everyone the Grace of forgiveness touches is restored to primordial innocence. Now you can see all things clearly. You are capable of wise action and clean communication, which can include holding your teenager to a standard of behavior or letting go of an employee who has crossed the line. Yet sweet love for others pervades your consciousness as you recognize them *as yourself.* A heavenly stream has found its way down to earth in your heart.

10 COMPASSION

Loving Your Suffering

You know quite well, deep within you,
There is only a single magic, a single power,
A single salvation—and that is called loving.
Very well then: love your suffering.
Do not resist it, do not flee from it.
It is your aversion that hurts, nothing else.

Often attributed to HERMAN HESSE

The transforming spiritual technology of forgiveness helps us navigate through the paradox of our inherent purity while simultaneously opening to the Grace that brings true correction. Forgiveness unwinds your grievances of feeling wronged by cleansing the heart and mind and preventing the recycling of hate and anger. Yet the etymology of the word *grievance* is "of grief." To truly heal, not just from loss but from anything that deeply hurts, we need the Grace of compassion. This is the healing balm that helps us address suffering—our own suffering, the suffering of those we love, and the suffering that pervades our world.

Since most of us find our way to the spiritual path motivated by the need to resolve some difficulty in our life, we can easily miss its transforming power to grow us. There is nothing that seasons our soul like turning the loving awareness of our heart toward what hurts. Yet opening to the transforming potential within fierce conditions runs counter to our survival instinct, which drives us toward pleasure and away from pain. How can we love our suffering? Why should we?

To paraphrase Franciscan priest and author Richard Rohr, spiritually, we grow the most through two things: great suffering and great love. While I pray for kind conditions for absolutely everyone, I am crisply aware that suffering can be a powerful crucible for awakening. Without passages of fierce Grace that brought me to my edges, requiring a total surrender, it is unlikely that these teachings would have arrived onto the page to share with you. Suffering can serve not just as an impetus for individual awakening but also for the awakening of whole cultures. Great collective psychological, social, and political evolution rose from the ashes of World War II's horrors and out of the turmoil of the 1960s. A quantum shift could arise out of the challenging times we live in now. It all hinges on our willingness to surrender into the invitations within suffering so we can listen and respond.

UNAVOIDABLE VS. UNNECESSARY SUFFERING

Suffering is part of the admission price of being human. It is a difficult fact of life that we will all grow old and meet loss, sickness, adversity, and the unexpected. When it is your turn to receive a challenging medical diagnosis or lose your job, your home, your money, or your marriage, it can feel like a personal punch in the gut. In times of adversity, you might rail, "Why me?" but really the question is, "Why *not* me?" As Pema Chödrön said, "[Pain and pleasure] are ordinary. Pain is not a punishment; pleasure is not a reward."[1] Nevertheless, we must meet the unavoidable sufferings of life with kindness and wisdom.

Yet so much unnecessary suffering, with its roots in ignorance of our true nature, pervades our world. The Buddha named this *dukka*, which loosely translates as "suffering" but more precisely means "being out of joint with your Self." I am sure you know exactly how it feels when you are out of joint with your deeper nature and suffer in some felt sense of disconnection, whether it be from real love, inherent value, peace, strength, or meaning. It can feel so demoralizing to find yourself recycling historical patterns of psychic pain, even after years of dedicated practice.

Even though your personal suffering may seem minor compared to that of many who do not have enough food, shelter, and clean water, it is important to compassionately address it, for everyone's sake. Any unresolved pattern of ignorance will cause you to relate and behave with unconscious self-centeredness. This will inevitably cause difficulties for others even when you are not intending it. Sometimes, even when you are aware of the impact of your unresolved suffering on others, you just cannot seem to stop. Transformation comes not through merely trying to transcend this but from a deeper meeting of the forces of your disconnection. We need love in these places like we need the oxygen in the next breath we take.

It takes great maturity to honestly and lovingly practice ego relaxation in the places where you fall short of your cherished ideals—not just to soothe yourself but to get to the roots that hold such patterns in place. Let them be touched by the living waters of Grace.

COMPASSION FOR YOUR EGO

One glorious summer afternoon, I was in session with Claire, a mature student. She sincerely wished for transformation from a chronic pattern of compulsively pushing herself. Not a newcomer to inquiry, Claire understood how this unkind mechanism had been laid down by internalizing her father's tough demeanor. Claire had worked through her dynamic with her father, and forgiveness had liberated past grievances. Yet she could not seem to stop this pushing, unkind way of treating herself that was now causing problems with her physical health.

That day, as she was lying on the mat, practicing ego relaxation in combination with breath work, an unmistakable healing breeze blew through her soul. I invited Claire to just be there, not rejecting the frustration, the hardness, the pushing, or the tightness she felt in her shoulders, neck, jaw, and mind. I suggested that she not try to get past this but rather turn toward it all with Absolute Love.

When you truly meet your most pernicious patterns all the way, you begin to see that you had no choice in how your ego defenses evolved. The fall from Grace we all go through in the first stage of life demands that we find a way to survive. Self-compassion can arise when you understand that the patterns you so wish were gone belong to a young self that feels so alone, so cut off from real love, power, peace, and support. From the vantage point of the awakened heart, our ego is a huge call for love. It was revelatory for Claire to love this frustrating pattern that had been such a font of suffering her whole life. Not only did the Grace of compassion arise, loosening the pattern, but it also ushered her into a new maturity.

COMPASSION IS MEETING RATHER THAN FIXING

It is natural to do whatever you practically can to make conditions kinder, yet often there are limitations to what you can do. Our ego tends to limit compassion to taking the pain away and fixing it as quickly as possible. The main problem with this surface view on compassion is that it gets in the way of letting the deeper transformational waters flow.

The first and most important step always is to remain as present as you can in the face of whatever is here. If you do not assume that suffering is inherently wrong, but make sensitive and kind contact with what hurts, just being there in the spirit of ego relaxation, the transforming power of Grace can emerge as true compassion. This is way more than a concept of kindness. Rather, it is a living presence that brings a soothing balm into our heart and onto the scene, like cooling aloe vera on sunburned skin. Healing arrives from realms beyond our mind, and in the process, it deepens our heart. Often it moves us to a greater understanding and empathy toward our fellow beings or births gifts that extend healing to others.

You might think, "I am being fully conscious of suffering because I am experiencing it." Sometimes there is a fine line between meeting suffering and wallowing in it. Meeting suffering is usually not that dramatic. Mostly, it is a soft, tender yielding to what is, with acceptance. *Truly loving your suffering means to stop defending against your own pain and even your own point of view.* This is the surrender of the heart. It is what opens up the vast heart.

Take a moment to reflect on an area in your life where there is some active suffering that confronts you personally. Perhaps it is some limitation that, despite years of practice, is still alive. Perhaps it is some great difficulty with your child, sister, brother, parent, or friend that you cannot fix. Perhaps you feel despair about the state of our world. Now, see what is arising as you have been reading this chapter—what feelings, thoughts, body sensations? How do you feel about this invitation to turn your heart toward, rather than away from, your suffering?

OBSTACLES TO LOVING YOUR SUFFERING

Typically, we meet three primary reactions when we turn toward our suffering. The most prevalent obstacle that arises is concern that if we contact suffering, we might be overwhelmed by the pain and collapse, unable to cope. Sometimes we fear it will pull us down into some dark, depressing pit from which there is no escape. Sadly, this is usually why many people stay away when someone they love is dying and why we might bury our heads in the sand and not listen to the news. It usually reveals a fear of not knowing what to do and thinking that that is a problem.

Remember your personality is not the source of compassion, is not the one who can meet it all. Compassion is a manifestation of Grace, and Grace always comes forward when you surrender, relax, and just be here—with nothing to fix or get or do. Your part is refusing to vacate the premises of your own heart. Feel your feet on the earth and your body held by the chair as you meet any concerns of overwhelm.

Another common concern is that if you contact the pain, you will get stuck. Since our ego believes it is the one that must make transformation happen, it can seem that if we do not actively resist or try to change the suffering, no transformation will take place. This is exactly the opposite of how the transforming power of Grace works. *It is impossible to let go of anything you are actively rejecting. It is your aversion that creates stuck-ness.* If relaxing your rejection feels like a big risk, remember what causes you to be here and trust in that.

Sometimes we have been resisting our suffering for so long that it has become part of our familiar way of knowing ourselves. Even when you sincerely want to be free, it can feel strangely disconcerting to drop the struggle against some force in yourself, or some force within the world. Part of popular spiritual teacher Byron Katie's "the Work" is asking the question, "Who would you be without this?" If you discover attachment to your suffering, just include it as part of what you open your heart toward.

ACCEPTING THE UNACCEPTABLE: TRANSFORMING PHYSICAL PAIN

Ultimately, transforming Grace comes whenever you find the capacity to accept what feels unacceptable. If you have ever had a serious injury or prolonged illness, then you know that living with unrelenting physical pain is fierce and rarely feels like Grace. It is always spiritually appropriate to reduce unnecessary suffering where possible, whether by medications or holistic treatments. However, given the escalating crisis of opioid addiction in our pain-averse society, I wonder whether we might have forgotten something fundamental. At the most basic level, pain is information. It asks us to listen, not just with our minds but with our senses, to what is truly needed. If we refuse to listen, we have no basis for wise responsiveness.

Yet if you open toward physical pain, which can feel so unacceptable at first, and practice ego relaxation with it, you begin to hear the invitations within the pain. Perhaps it nudges you to sit differently, stretch more, back off that inflammatory food, rest when you are exhausted, or seek a different approach. Contacting and listening to pain empowers you to trust your body's wisdom. This helps you navigate the best course of action in the face of conflicting medical advice.

There is no question that ego relaxation is hardest to practice when we hurt. Yet often we do not see how we are compounding physical suffering with our minds every time we insist, "This should not be." Many people with serious physical limitations have reported a dramatic difference in their pain levels through the practice of ego relaxation. Many have even experienced healings. The more your consciousness relaxes and lets go of rejecting what is, the more the homeostatic forces of healing can arrive in body, heart, and mind.

LOVING ONE ANOTHER THROUGH SUFFERING

Mysteriously, as I was writing this chapter, my beloved husband was suddenly struck down by a serious spinal infection. My normally robust, vital man was rendered unable to walk, think straight, or do anything much for himself. In the blink of an eye, I became a full-time caregiver, doing everything I could to get his untenable pain under control and navigate through a complex medical journey. He would wake in the early hours of the night in agony, helpless and afraid. I did everything I possibly could to help him. However, often nothing seemed to help. I could but stay there, as love, doing what could be done. My heart felt as though it was not just the size of my chest but the size of the whole house.

Within these fierce conditions, I began to feel such selflessness that we all hope is the truth of our love for another but never know for certain until it is tested. I felt such empathy for every parent who has had to watch their child burn through a fever, not knowing whether it would break, and for every husband who has held his wife's hand through the ravages of cancer and eventually had to let her go. While it was so hard, I could also feel it carving out something new in my soul.

When someone you love is suffering, and you cannot ease it, there is a mystical power that comes if you can just *be* there, doing what you can, even when it does not seem to change the situation much. This demands that you learn to stay present and open through your own limitations. If you can feel but not react against helplessness, the transforming power of Grace can emerge through you, bringing a new synthesis of love and healing power.

LOVING OUR COLLECTIVE SUFFERING

Transforming Grace can find us in the fierce conditions we meet collectively also. Five days into the fires that devastated Sonoma County in Northern California, the meeting hall of my local ongoing *sangha* (spiritual community) was full, with many having traveled through dangerous smoky conditions to be together. As we began to chant the Om Namah Shivaya mantra and drop into silence together, the power of our shared presence was more palpable than I had ever experienced. Our hearts had been broken open by the situation, feeling such empathy for those who had lost everything.

Neurotic concerns gave way to a new depth of humanity, expressing as deep kindness, kinship, willingness to open hearts and homes, and share what resources we had to help our fellow human beings. Witnessing this transformation in group consciousness made me hopeful that the evolution our world so needs will likely bypass our politicians, emerging instead from the ground up, from ordinary human beings able to stay present, meet pain, and let loving, wise response come.

MEETING SUFFERING AS A SPIRITUAL INITIATION

As I sit with suffering, be it within myself or with those I love or listening to the daily horrors presented via the news each night, I am reminded of the archetype of the women at the passion of Christ. The conventional gospels present Mary Magdalene, Mother Mary, and Elizabeth as well as John at the foot of the cross. All the other known disciples had fled, either because they could not bear witness to the loss and injustice or because they feared for their own safety. Some of the gnostic gospels tell of there being many other women present on the scene.

The transforming Grace of compassion has an inherently feminine quality to it—whether we inhabit a male or female body. Our heart becomes a birthing chamber for something deeper than our personality, like a womb bringing new life into the world. There is a Sufi *dkihr* (devotional practice) that I learned within the Inayati Order many years ago that repeated, "Out of the womb of the human heart, God is born."

The women at the foot of the cross were embodying the essence of true compassion. They stayed present *as* love, even in the face of impossible suffering for which they could practically do nothing. While Christ was undergoing his final surrender, perhaps Mary Magdalene was being spiritually initiated as well, deepening her capacity to receive Christ in his risen form, preparing the others to accept what must have blown their minds. The transforming power of Grace can harness the most impossible situations we face on our human journey to bring us to a whole new platform of reality.

GARGOYLES ON THE GATE TO THE SANCTUARY

I once lived in the medieval university town of Oxford, England, and was always amused by the scary faces that were built into the walls of exterior buildings and were thought to scare off evil spirits. One would never know that behind many of these walls were often the most serene, beautiful courtyards and resplendent gardens of roses and jasmine.

Similarly, when you contact suffering directly, you might contact some physical or psychic pain; you may meet sadness, hurt, or frustration. You may encounter limitations, but something surprising and beautiful begins to unfold. As your aversion melts, you begin to see that at the core of even our unnecessary suffering, nothing is wrong. Your ego is not the demon, not wrong. However, *your ego mechanisms are not you; they are a structure you have taken to be yourself.* This is why our practice of ego relaxation is so very effective. It just invites you, again and again, to "be nothing, do nothing, get nothing, become nothing, seek for nothing, relinquish nothing. Be as you are. Rest in God."

HEALING HAPPENS BY GRACE

Ultimately, it is not up to us when or how suffering is liberated. It happens by Grace, and Grace finds us the more we learn to let go *into* what is. When we finally just accept our situation, see our limitations and patterns honestly, and meet the various layers of pain—*with and from love*—the gates open. Grace brings forth the healing qualities, or some wisdom that supports healing, and all of a sudden, we are underneath the unnecessary suffering of "I and mine."

Your challenges may stay or change, but you are not so attached to your concepts of what should be happening. As you surrender even into the difficult forces of life, you grow deeper, wiser, more fully human. You become kinder to your limitations while being more truthful about them. This makes you more compassionate with everyone else.

The more you practice ego relaxation with what hurts, continuing to surrender into a larger field of intelligence, the more you recognize that we are all in the hands of Grace, always, and that we have never been in charge, despite our delusions of control. Our capacity to meet the sufferings and complexities in our world expands, and the living waters flow more fully through us.

I invite you to journey deeper using the following inquiry and meditation exercises.

INQUIRY **Opening to Self-Compassion**

Let the following questions enter into your heart, your body, and your awareness. Let whatever comes come, without editing or judging. See if you can be detailed in your responses, as this will greatly expand your inquiry.

What is most difficult for you to stay present with and feel?
Perhaps it's an ego pattern that you most wish was not there, some physical pain, or the suffering of a loved one. Name something, then move to the next question.

What does your aversion provide that you think you need?
When it comes, say "thank you" to it, and move to the next question.

What do you truly need to stay present and open into this all the way?
Cycle back through these three questions. Only proceed to the next question after you have cycled through this sequence for at least ten minutes.

Now, explore this question for a further ten to fifteen minutes: *What's it like in body, heart, and mind if you open your heart to your own limitations?* Live into this question, taking it with you on walks in nature and into the moments when you find frustration, pain, or difficulty. Let the transforming power of Grace live in your heart *as* compassion. ~

MEDITATION **The Grace of Compassion**

This is a beautiful practice to steep in when there is suffering to be borne, whether because of something you are running up against in yourself or with a loved one, or even if you find your heart sinking while watching the news.

1. Settle into your sacred space and begin with the Ground in the Mountain of Presence meditation (chapter 3). Stay with this until you start to feel a sense of being grounded in Grace.

2. Feel and see that shower of light, perhaps calling upon a name or face of the Divine that you love best (as in chapter 7). See on your crown that hand of light that brings blessings and sustenance beyond this world. Feel yourself *in* and *part of* that light that claims you as its own. Stay with this as long as you need to.

3. Bring your awareness to the heart. Feel each breath allowing more and more space to emerge so that you start to gain deeper access to the depth of heart that is deeper than "yours" and "mine."

4. Feel as if you are naturally backing into the heart-cave that we explored in the previous chapter. Be open to however this appears to you, focusing on opening into the pure love/pure being that *is* the heart.

5. Ask for help and healing with anything you need. Feel the heart-cave welcoming all that is vulnerable, difficult,

and painful. Feel it welcoming you in your entirety to rest here. Let the suffering you do not know how to deal with just rest here. Remember that the vast heart has your back.

6. Compassionate beings or a healing presence might emerge; these do not belong to any personality. Be open to however they arrive, and let them pervade you.

7. Let the compassionate presence breathe you and breathe through you. Stay present as love with all that is difficult, with all that you do not understand, with all that does not seem to make sense. If you vow not to leave the heart, the transforming presence of true compassion can never leave you. ~

Sometimes healing is needed before you can let go into deeper dimensions of consciousness. Loving your suffering helps you practice ego relaxation with whatever is happening in life so you can just settle kindly and relax your resistance to what is. Freed from clinging and avoiding, you can stay present and meet everything with love as your mind dissolves back into God. This readies you for a powerful dive through and beyond the construct of your primary ego identity.

11 UNWINDING YOUR CORE EGO IDENTITY

Your true nature is that of infinite spirit.
The feeling of limitation is the work of the mind.
When the mind unceasingly investigates its own nature,
It transpires that there is no such thing as mind.
This is the direct path for all.

SRI RAMANA MAHARSHI, ***Be as You Are: The Teachings of Sri Ramana Maharshi*** **(edited by David Godman)**

Now that we have opened to the purifying presence of forgiveness and the healing, humanizing balm of true compassion, we can allow Grace to unwind the greatest block to living love and freedom: our core ego identity. Even after significant awakening, it is humbling how easy it is to loop back into the painful pit you might recognize as some variation of "I'm not enough." The transforming power of Grace wants to harness the energy within your most pernicious knot of suffering as a launching pad to the infinite. Your part in this transformation is to drop in and through the very thing you have spent a lifetime trying to avoid.

To be clear, ego itself is not the enemy. If you want to fly from San Francisco to London and have your suitcase arrive at your destination, you will need an identity tag that has your name and address on it. Likewise, your body and even your personality can become a more graceful vehicle for life. Just as the force of water will eventually smooth out the rough edges of a rock, your personality becomes more transparent to its true nature, less crudely "egocentric," from ongoing engagement in practices like those in this book. The goal is not to stamp out the personality and become some depersonalized, disassociated "nobody." Rather, the goal is to loosen the *fixations* of your personality to relax the Mini-Me in your mind that is the root cause of unhappiness.

Here is the good news: you are way deeper than you realize. As Roberto Assagioli, founder of psychosynthesis, points out, "I have a body, but I am not my body. I have an emotional life, but I am not my emotions or feelings."[1] Neither are you your gender, opinions, political affiliation, job, or role in life. Authentically shifting your center of gravity requires first recognizing that your familiar way of knowing yourself is not ontologically real. The central character in your movie is a self-image: a structure made of memories, conclusions, preferred emotional states, and attachments that you call "me."

When you identify with what author Neal Rogin calls your "prisonality," you cannot help but recycle limiting patterns.[2] You will relate to the spiritual path as a way to fix your perceived problems or harness luminous practices and teachings merely to soothe yourself. It is time to stop rearranging the deck chairs on the *Titanic*. Instead, bring all of your perceived problems to the one true solution—unwinding the script upon which your story of "me" is written.

TAKING OFF THE CRACKED GLASSES

Imagine that you were wearing a pair of cracked glasses, only you did not know you had them on. Everything you saw would be distorted. You would react emotionally and even physically to all kinds of things that are not ultimately real, frightening yourself and causing all manner of unnecessary strife. Yet the trouble originates from the fact that you do not realize you are looking through a cracked lens. Ramana Maharshi said, "Just as the spider emits the thread (of its web) out of itself and then withdraws it, so you emit a world out of your mind."[3] The transforming power of Grace is not about helping you fix the cracks; it's about helping you take off the cracked glasses. Only then can you wake up to a whole new world.

One blustery December afternoon, I drove to the hospital to sit with Sandy, a longtime student who was coming out of surgery. She had been battling breast cancer for seventeen years, yet recently the disease was becoming more aggressive.

Sandy had sat in regular sessions with me for four years prior to this moment. Our primary focus was unwinding layers of anxiety laid down like train tracks in her mind and body from repeated incidences of abuse and neglect in her childhood. Sandy was a longtime meditator and no fool. However, she struggled to get past the need to seek evidence that she was unsafe and uncared for. Her mind was tenaciously attached to its version of reality, centered in the script "I'm unlovable," which drove a cluster of tricky defense strategies.

At the hospital that day, it was completely different. The morphine was inhibiting not just Sandy's physical pain but also her ego's filter on reality. The usual suspicion was gone, and Sandy perceived me as some angel radiating all the love in the universe. She kept uttering, "There's so much love," over and over again. I held her hand and softly directed Sandy's attention deeper with simple questions like, "What's it like to feel this all-pervasive love? Where does it seem to begin and end? Who is this one sensing this love? How does the world appear from here?"

Accepting my prompts minus the usual resistance, Sandy discovered that she *was* the boundless sea of love she was experiencing, in which all is always well and there is no cause for fear. Soaring into nondual reality minus any historically based filters, Sandy could witness the patterns of her familiar personality, yet without identifying with them. There was natural compassion and forgiveness for all the central characters of her past. This precious encounter into her true nature lasted about an hour.

Then, seemingly out of nowhere, a poison arrow seemed to shoot through Sandy's mind, closing the curtains on the boundless love she had been in and part of. Her breath tightened; her face pinched into tense lines and furrows. The muscles of her neck, arms, and mouth contracted. I was witnessing the reconstellation of an ego identity in slow motion.

Sandy's script of "I'm unlovable" came back online. Anxiety arrived, along with anger and blame. Familiar defenses clicked into full gear, haranguing the nurses with agitated words: "I need this, I want that, don't do that, you're not doing it right," presuming they were as incompetent or uncaring as her mother had been.

My attempts to settle Sandy, encouraging her to trust the medical team and receive their competent care, went completely ignored. Her ego identity had reasserted its dominance, distorting her vision with those cracked glasses. Now, she was actively blocking the love and support that was present, while demanding to get her needs met and fighting everyone around her. This whole painful display was taking place in her mind.

Driving home that night, I found it resoundingly clear that a process like this occurs within each of us every morning as we supposedly "wake up." However, really it is the opposite. While our body is coming out of the sleep state, our familiar identity is reifying itself—pulling together the threads of its web on which we live our life. We call it "reality," but often it is the wild projections—the cracked glasses—of our mind, recycling needless stories of suffering.

WHAT'S YOUR BRAND?

Ego identification is the end result of a process of falling from Grace into the state of separation. This happens to us all in the first stage of our life. Yet we each experience this fall in a unique way, which is influenced by our early environment and perhaps previous lives. We draw conclusions about who we are, how the world is, and what we must do to survive. This forms the scaffolding of our personality structure and creates our unconscious ego activity. Until we see these layers fully for what they are and get to know our Self deeper than our personality, they become the patterns that shape our lives.

Consider some pattern that, despite your best efforts, you have not been able to get past. Perhaps it is a repeating cycle of disappointment in your intimate relationships, a struggle with kindly caring for your body, a holding back from expressing yourself authentically, a pattern of conflict avoidance, a difficulty navigating finances and practical details, or a challenge of being consistent and following through. Take a moment to reflect on what limiting pattern is knocking on your inner door. Be with it compassionately as you read on.

Being caught in any limiting pattern feels painful and frustrating. You feel deficient and lacking, like a small insecure child. Forgetting that your personal stream of experience is happening within God, you seem disconnected from the love, peace, joy, clarity, strength, value, and meaning—the very qualities of your true nature. It is no joke.

DISCRIMINATING YOUR EXPERIENCE OF SEPARATION

I am sure you know very well how it feels when love seems absent and when you feel you do not have intrinsic value. You feel anxious, shaky, ungrounded. Your solar plexus tightens, and your body, heart, and mind contract. You are compelled then to *do* something—anything—to get love and affirmation of your value from the outside. However, whatever strategy you reach for never quite does the job because it is a compensatory work-around of a young child.

Perhaps the qualities you become most separated from are a sense of strength, capacity, and confidence. Perhaps separation for you feels like being disconnected from joy, peace, or any sense of meaning. Perhaps you feel separate from all of the above qualities. Imagine being very young and feeling this disconnection for the first time; it literally triggers a fight-or-flight response in your body and a great contraction in your heart and mind.

Victor Frankl, author of *Man's Search for Meaning*, illuminated that our survival instinct drives us to create meaning out of our experience. He called this method, born of his study of Holocaust survivors, "logotherapy." As a young child, every time you felt separate, whether from love, value, meaning, joy, strength, or peace, you could not help but arrive at a conclusion about *why* this was happening. It is a way we contextualize our experiences into some kind of meaningful narrative.

Since we are dependent on our caregivers, we need to think that they are "right," even when they are operating through their own undigested distortions, as is often the case. Thus as young children, we conclude that the reason we might not be receiving the understanding, love, kindness, support, attention, or guidance that we need is because of something *we* lack. Thus our core ego identity is born: "I'm (fill in the blank)."

THE EGO'S GREATEST HITS

Not yet understanding that our parents have limitations that have nothing to do with us and that are no one's fault, we tend to conclude, "I'm not good enough," "I'm flawed," "I'm bad," I'm wrong," "I'm unlovable," "I'm worthless," "I don't matter," or "I'm nothing" when our needs are not met. It feels like we have descended into our personal hell.

Whatever the tune of your ego identity, it feels as if we must keep this hidden at all costs, imagining that we are the only ones experiencing such a shameful deficiency. Most people spend their whole life trying to overcompensate, fix, or transcend feeling insufficient, flawed, or empty. This is the root cause of most of the ugly behavior on our planet. Covering up our ego deficiency produces arrogance, insatiable greed, addictions, and most forms of burnout, not to mention depression. Take a few minutes to just breathe, sense your body, and vow not to leave yourself right here and now.

The real problem is that we identify with our brand of "I'm (fill in the blank)" as a fact rather than recognizing it as the *conclusions of a young child who did not have the full picture*. Identifying with your brand sets off a tidal wave of ego activity, chasing after what you believe you do not have, while rejecting the qualities that are always present. Feeding what Buddhism calls the "hungry ghost of craving and aversion" sends you spinning deeper into your story and then frantically trying to fix it. This is akin to sitting in a movie theater and shouting directions at actors on the screen.

IDENTITY DRIVES YOUR AUTOMATIC DEFENSES

Anna, one of my diligent students, was courageously exploring her ego identity of "I'm bad" in a private session. She recognized this as the driving force behind repeating patterns of rejection, feeling treated as an outsider, trying so hard to be "good," and alternately acting out through reckless behavior with substances and sexuality. Anna begged the question, "How do I get beyond this?"

I asked Anna the question that I have since posed to all my students: "When you identify with 'I'm bad,' what typically do you *do*?"

With touching honesty, Anna rattled off some behaviors you might recognize: "I go to the fridge and see what I can eat," "I surf the web and buy things I don't need," "I watch Netflix until I pass out," "I ruminate on who I am upset with and pick a fight with them in my mind," "I bury myself in work so I don't have to feel it," "I get my vibrator out," and more. Anna saw how all of these activities were ways to try to change her agitated state by *rejecting* what is and *grasping* for something else. She saw how so much of her ordinary daily activity involved leaving herself. Furthermore, she saw that every defensive action reified her core ego identity of "I'm bad."

Consider what happens when you do not stop to question your personal script of separation. What do you typically do to try to soothe or escape your state? This is the place where you most need to practice ego relaxation—just being here, feeling everything, but doing nothing.

THE "PROBLEM" IS THE GATE

Reflecting back over my decades of spiritual practice, it is now clear that like so many sincere seekers, I was engaging in spiritual practices to offset, transcend, or fix the seeming problem of "me." My version revolved around an inner identity of "I'm nothing," backed by a long history of feeling unseen, unvalued, and unsupported. Energetically, it felt as if I had a giant hole inside that left me feeling deficient, insecure, and valueless, even though I knew intellectually this was not true. Still, it would gnaw away at me, inhibiting any sense of ease, driving me to prove myself valuable, worthwhile, and special. This lent itself to depressive tendencies and a great deal of overcompensation, including spiritual overcompensation.

I would never have guessed that the doorway to the freedom I had been seeking my entire life would come through softly relaxing into being "nothing." By Grace, that day I sat on the dusty old cushion in Ramana Maharshi's cave, I was not trying to fix myself. I was not seeking any bells or whistles. I was just happy to be quiet and sit. Now it seems like some great cosmic joke that the very thing I thought was my biggest problem turned out to be the gate.

It was miraculous to open to the truth of "I'm nothing" and let all of my ego compensations go, to just be here, not trying to be special, different, or better. By Grace, I dropped through my own self-image, and with the disappearance of "me" and "story" came the disappearance of a fearful world. I now understand why this had such power to shift my center of gravity so substantially. It can for us all.

As the Advaita giant Nisargadatta Maharaj points out: "It is always the false that makes you suffer, the false desires and fears, the false values and ideas, the false relationships between people. Abandon the false and you are free of pain: truth makes happy, truth liberates."[4]

THE TRUTH OF EGO DEFICIENCY

Sharing this teaching with people across the boundaries of age, culture, and profession, I have yet to meet someone who does not relate intimately to this material. This is because all ego structures, even those that belong to people who appear confident, are fundamentally insecure at the core.

There is some truth to the matter: our ego, taking itself to be a separate someone, actually *is* limited! It is a shell busily trying to imitate the real thing, which is Infinite Being, or God. This need not be a cause for shame and need not set you on a self-improvement journey. Seeing the truth of "I'm nothing" or "I'm not enough" is actually cause for a great celebration. It means that you can relax the effort of trying to shore your ego up. Retire from that hard work of trying to fight off something that is nothing more than the inevitable distortion produced by a cracked pair of glasses.

Transforming Grace can arrive when you admit the truth of your ego's limitations and accept the futility of your defenses to ever fully work. *Cease protecting* your ego deficiency. Instead, just meet it for what it is. You will not die from staying present and feeling the truth of "nothing" or "not enough." While it is not fun to feel vulnerable, helpless, or unseen, you can relax into the ground of Grace, by which you are always supported, as well as receive and recognize the blessings of Grace just as you receive the light of the sun. Your familiar "me" might feel "I'll die," but remember: only your self-image can die, and that is very good news.

DROPPING *IN* AND *THROUGH* YOUR EGO IDENTITY

What if you could truly feel, face, and sense into the limitation of "me" and just do nothing? I do not mean collapse or check out in some avoidant way, but explore freshly what is truly here when you are no longer defending or compensating for your brand of ego deficiency. When you are no longer telling a story about who you are, you can explore, "What's here?" and "Who's here?"

This is not some intellectual exercise, and it cannot be led by your mind. Yet with sincere devotion and willingness, you can drop right in and through that which you have most tried to skirt around. This is one of the most important surrenders of the spiritual path, and it grants you access into boundless realms. It has the potential to substantially shift your core center of gravity, bringing a game-changing transformation. As always, the transformer is Grace itself.

The following is a powerful sequence of inquiry questions designed to help you discriminate your core ego identity. Before your core ego identity can be transformed, it must be seen and understood. This can help you harness a reactive pattern into a gateway for freedom. Ideally, follow the inquiry with the meditation that follows so you not only gain the discriminating awareness of your ego identity but also drop energetically through and beyond it. Engage these two practices any time you feel bound in your story.

INQUIRY **Unwinding Your Core Ego Identity**

To begin, settle yourself using the basic Ego Relaxation practice (chapter 1). In your own way, prayerfully call upon support from any enlightened being you feel a connection with, perhaps seeing a hand of light on your crown. Ask for all subtle support to be with you as you journey deeply into the following questions.

Name a limiting pattern that manifests in your life.
It does not matter what it is, only that you sincerely wish to open to some transformation with it. Choose *one* thing!

Where does this manifest?
In your body? Your relationships? Your professional life? Your friendships? Your spiritual practice? The practical structures of your life? It might appear in multiple areas.

How does this make you feel?
Be open to both emotional and somatic feelings.

How old do you feel in this pattern?
This is not necessarily about memories, but rather notice what "age" you feel when this pattern gets activated.

What do you feel separate from in this?
What qualities of true nature feel like they are just not available? Love? Inherent value? Strength? Capacity? Joy? Meaning? Peace? Clarity? A combination? Be specific.

What do you make this mean about who you are?
This is your ego brand: "I'm (fill in the blank)." You will know you are in touch with this by the feeling of being ground into a contracted and familiar pit. Be mindful to discriminate between an *experience*, like feeling you are "rejected" or "abandoned," and a *conclusion*, which is what you make that experience of rejection or abandonment *mean* about who you *are*. Here, your objective is to see how you turn an experience of separation into a personal identity.

When you identify with "I'm (fill in the blank)," what do you do?
How do you *grasp* for something else, *reject* what is, and *leave* the present?

What does all of this help you avoid?
Be open to what comes, as you might be surprised.

What is this all happening within?
Notice the space in which all of this is occurring. Again, be open, as you might be surprised. ~

MEDITATION **Dropping Through and Beyond Your Ego Identity**

This meditation practice is a continuation of the inquiry sequence above. It is designed to help you harness the insights as well as the bound energy within your ego identity as a gateway to who you are at a deeper level than "me." This is the practice you want to turn to whenever you feel stuck or get tripped up in a repetitive, limiting pattern of suffering.

1. Take a moment to reflect on what you have discovered about your core ego identity and the limiting pattern you wish to transform.

2. Ground in the Mountain of Presence practice (chapter 3). Sense your lower body in contact with the ground and melt in and down with each exhale, into that felt sense that you are infinitely supported and held by something way beyond your mind. Stay with this until you feel that you have a stable base in the ground of Grace.

3. Consciously welcome the support of subtle forces of Grace, calling upon the enlightened beings, bodhisattvas, or angels to come dynamically forward in your experience. Ask for an inner guide for this journey and trust who appears. You *will* be responded to; just be open, as you might be surprised. It might just feel like a loving presence arriving in your heart or a hand of light on your crown. You might see the face of an enlightened being or someone from your past whom you felt unconditionally accepted by. If nothing else, know that I am right here with you.

4. Consider all the beings on the planet who are caught in a similar cycle of suffering, of identifying with "I'm unlovable," "I'm not good enough," "I'm bad," and "I'm weak." Dedicate the fruits of this journey to the liberation of all who stumble in a similar way.

5. Feel, sense, or see this loving guide inviting you into an inner elevator. Feel yourself dropping in and down inside, to the basement of your consciousness—that ancient place where you feel most limited, lacking, deficient, or separate, that place you most want to avoid. Just be here and breathe. Nothing you need to do.

6. Open toward everything you find. Open especially to that which you have most wanted to push past. Feel the loving presence here with you and explore the various layers of your inner content afresh.

7. Open toward feelings and sensations. Perhaps you notice fear, insecurity, shame, anger, weakness, powerlessness, or vulnerability. Notice the energy in your body, notice the sensations, and notice how old you feel. Just be here and breathe. There's nothing you need to do.

8. Open toward whoever appears in your ego basement. Perhaps it's Mother, Father, siblings, or significant people from your past. Who else was involved in shaping your identity of "I'm (fill in the blank)"? Don't go seeking; just see what unfolds and open toward it. Just be here and breathe. Nothing you need to do.

9. Open toward your drive to shut down, run away, grasp, and make it different. But instead of letting the defenses rule, open into the energy within them. It's like staying with a difficult yoga pose—just be here and breathe. Nothing you need to do.

10. Whoever and whatever appears in your basement, open toward it with love. If memories come, let them come. If your body shakes, gets hot or cold, or tears come, let it all be. Vow not to abandon your direct experience. Just be here with love, meeting everything, doing nothing.

11. Stay with all that you find until it starts to empty out. You might find that "others" integrate into you or disappear. Stay with everything until there is a sense of transparency.

12. See and sense the basement walls and floor becoming transparent and then disappearing. Your inner perception opens into the infinite vast space, where there are no walls, no floor, no other, and no self-construct.

13. Open, soften, and stretch into the space itself. Do not cling to anything you have learned before. Rest in the space of humble not-knowing.

14. Sense into the vast space that exists prior to any definition. You might notice a felt sense of being in the infinite expanse of the universe.

15. Now, what's shining in the deeper basement of your being? Who are you here?

If you sincerely take your time with this inquiry and meditation, it is possible for you to discover that what shines in the deeper basement of your being is *you*. However, it is not some historically based, limited, shame-filled version of personality, but a luminous presence of infinite beauty. ~

A Course in Miracles says: "The truth in you remains as radiant as a star, as pure as light, as innocent as love itself."[5] Conceptually affirming this is not enough, but meeting the layers of your ego identity and dropping in and through it allows the transforming power of Grace to dissolve the limiting structures. Like Moses opening to the Grace that parted the Red Sea, you cross over the shore of your ego "me" to discover a whole new land of freedom—a land not bound by the brand "I'm (fill in the blank)" but alight in "I *am*."

12 RESTING IN BOUNDLESS TRUE NATURE

Consider all the pain and all the pleasure
You have ever experienced
As waves on a very deep ocean which you are.

From the depths, witness those waves,
Rolling along so bravely, always changing,
Beautiful in their self-sustaining power.

Marvel that once, you identified with
Only the surface of this ocean.
Now embrace the waves, depths, undersea mountains,
Out to the farthest shore.

LORIN ROCHE, ***The Radiance Sutras***

The more you discriminate the layers of your ego identity and meet the misperception, hurts, and history with love while doing nothing to change or fix it, the more your sense of being a limited, separate somebody starts to dissolve. This opens inner space from which the transforming power of Grace can come dynamically alive. Not only does it lift you *out of* the separate "me" story that keeps you bound in your patterns of suffering, it also lifts you *into* an infinite expanse. As the curtains of your consciousness open, you discover pristine being, pure awareness, boundless love, and so much more. Transformation occurs not only from experiencing these boundless realms but also from recognizing this luminosity as who you truly are.

Sometimes the loftiest openings have the greatest practical power to change not only your inner experience but also our world. Whenever you insist that the appearance of separation is a fact rather than, as Dzogchen teachings describe it, "multiple displays in the one fabric of Being," you suffer unnecessarily. Your inner eyes are closed to the truth that what you want and need is always here, sewn into the very fabric of your being. Your innate gifts and capacities remain locked behind closed doors. It is time to reclaim your spiritual inheritance, adjust to a significantly expanded view of reality, and let it become a new platform from which to live your life.

RESTING *IN* AND AS PART OF GOD

Inevitably, we all launch on the inner journey from the perspective of a separate "me" who wants to come home. In the ancient Sumerian myth, the queen Inanna lets go of her worldly garments and embarks on a journey into the underworld because she hears the cries of her long-lost sister whom she has never met. Whether your path was originally prompted by the need to resolve some problem or suffering or whether it appeared mysteriously, it is a great blessing not only that you heard the call but that you were compelled to answer it.

The more you engage in authentic practices and teachings, the more you naturally start to contact the inner luminosity. You feel seduced into prayer, meditation, contemplation—anything that helps you walk *with* Divine Presence, as if in a spiritual partnership. You feel carried by a Grace that is in you but not of you.

Ultimately, as Francis of Assisi reportedly said, "The one you are looking for is the one who is looking." This nondual shift beyond identifying with "me" as the subject—relating to the Divine, the path, and everything beyond the borders of your mind and body as "object"—is a crucial turning point. You recognize that all of your seeking and praying and stumbling has been happening *within* God. This recognition has the power to substantially expand your view on reality, as if you are seeing the landscape of your life from the vantage point of a high mountain peak.

As patterned perception opens into unified vision, expanded resources and capacities emerge that you did not know were buried inside. Everything starts to feel vast, magical, and shimmering with potential. Who would have guessed that the true resolution to lifetimes of struggle is getting to know who you really are underneath all of your dusty old garments? Yet you cannot force this shift in identity. The transforming power of Grace dances with your sincerity of practice but to its own mysterious time signature.

You might have tried meditating into the perennial spiritual question "Who am I?" As we explored in the previous chapter, this classical jnana yoga inquiry will first expose your attachments, helping discriminate who you are not. It will show where you have drawn the internal boundaries of "me" and "not me." You may bump into inherent qualities of true nature, like love, peace, spaciousness, and clarity. You may see these qualities as having no beginning, middle, or end. However, answering the question with "I am love" or "I am pure consciousness" comes close, but it does not quite satisfy. This is because who you truly are contains all the divine qualities but is beyond the particularity of any one quality.

BEYOND YOUR MENTAL BOUNDARIES

Before launching deeper into the boundless, it is important to remember that on the ordinary level of reality, boundaries have their rightful place. Even when you know you are not a body or a mind, not bound by time or a past, and ultimately not separate from anyone, it is still important to keep your word and to be respectful of others' property, time, and feelings. It is especially important to respect natural energetic and sexual boundaries. It causes carnage when we misuse nondual teachings to confuse the levels of relative and Absolute reality, to skirt around being decent people.

It is our mental boundaries that we want to dissolve. This can include anything that your ego has amassed to build a fixed sense of self upon, fencing off "me" from "not me." As integral philosopher Ken Wilber points out, "As an individual draws up the boundaries of his soul, he establishes at the same time the battles of his soul."[1] Mental boundaries can include beliefs, trauma patterns, attachments, roles, and assumptions, from our personal journey and also our ancestral and cultural inheritance. Much of this lives in our unconscious, and it is why we need ongoing support from like-minded friends and ideally a spiritual mentor. Everything that binds our identity in a sense of separation wants to be met with love so our life force can be freed up.

When your identification with "I'm (fill in the blank)" genuinely gives way to the spaciousness of "I *am*," it feels unspeakably beautiful. You feel as though you are truly home, washed clean from the past by the living waters. The dense ego features of fear, judgment, control, and self-centeredness evaporate. Pride, anger, and grievances have no cause. However, it can also feel a bit disorienting. Many people report feeling "woozy," as if they are about to disappear down the rabbit hole. This sense of disorientation is the felt experience of your mental boundaries letting go. In moments like these, the key is to relax and let it happen. Go ahead and dissolve. Let the walls come down.

VULNERABILITY MAKES YOU TRANSPARENT TO GRACE

As all that you thought defined you in concrete time, form, and location starts to give way, it can challenge not just your sense of self but everything you thought was real. Inevitably, this can make you feel profoundly vulnerable at first. Mercifully, this dissolving does not usually happen all at once. More commonly, it happens in small chunks, like sections of an ice pack that melt and flow back into the fluid freedom of the spring waterfall. This itself is a gift of Grace because it helps you adjust to a new paradigm gradually.

When I sit with students exploring who they truly are underneath all construct, they often report seeing my face change and seeing forms in the room disappear, as if all that is fixed and dense begins to morph and become transparent. Many report feeling as if they are hanging in infinite space. We need the spiritual musculature developed in the earlier chapters of meeting fear, melting control, and cultivating trust, humility, and patience so we can just be here, doing nothing. Remember that whatever you leave empty, Grace can fill.

It is easier to practice ego relaxation in some situations than others. It is humbling to discover how attached we can be to our familiar way of knowing ourselves and our familiar way of viewing the world even though we know both are limited and cause suffering. Like a young child attached to its transitional object of a comfort blanket or doll, we cling to what we know to help our ego feel secure. This is why we need self-forgiveness and compassion as we live into ongoing surrender.

Ego relaxation invites you to be present and undefended with everything, and that includes the more subtle experiences as well as vulnerability, fear, and resistance. Inevitably, with patience and persistence, you recognize that everything you see, feel, and experience is also *part of you*. With this dawning realization, beholding faces morphing and hanging out in unknown spaces is no longer frightening but quite wondrous. Carlos Castaneda called this a shift in our "assemblage point." As your mental boundaries fall away, it feels as if "you" are everywhere, not contained within the borders of your physical body. You are *in* everything that you see and simultaneously *the one* who is seeing it all. Do not settle for just a little more peace and happiness on the side. Grace wants to give you the keys to the kingdom.

UNITY OPENS INFINITE POSSIBILITY

In the Book of John, Jesus says, "My father's house hath many mansions."[2] I read this not merely as reassurance that Jesus is going to prepare the way for the faithful in the next realm but that he is speaking of the heavenly boundless realms of Grace, which become available to us when we let go of all that we think we are and all that we think the world is, when we simply come and come again with wholly empty hands unto God.

Most contemporary nondual teachers emphasize our true identity as pure awareness aware of itself, but why limit the possibilities to only one flavor? Why not continue opening to our boundless true nature as having "many mansions"? This perspective can turn your practice into a grand unfolding adventure. It supports you to remain humble and open to be taught directly by nonconceptual Grace what truly is and how, therefore, to live a beautiful and meaningful life in each unfolding moment.

The less you cling to any position and any prior subtle experience, the more gnosis comes online. Your crown chakra, which the Vedas state has one thousand petals, can dial in to a divine radio station from which it is possible to receive the logic, light, and transmission of higher realms. The more you abide in the unified condition, the more you can "know" without anyone having to teach you. It can feel like streams of insight pouring through body, heart, and mind, like light pours through a clean window. It defies the need for linear conceptual learning, for you are now open to what Kabbalists call "Ein Sof"—the pure light of God.

I am often asked what my preparation process for teaching is—where all these inquiry questions and meditations come from. It is very simple: I sit at my altar and bow to the mystery. I give homage to all of my teachers and their teachers. I open with gratitude to the Grace of Ramana and the celestial beings I sense. Then I simply settle into the silence and empty out. I rest into being nothing and no one. I simply rest in That which *is*. Then I contemplate my students. While I know they are not separate from me, in the realm of form, it seems there is a role to fulfill, something to be shared. I open even to those I have not yet met, like you, dear reader. I do not presume to know anything. Like dropping a penny into a still pond, I ask, "What's needed?" and sit in receptivity. When I'm not trying to grab hold of anything, the stream of Grace begins to unfold, often even before I have asked the question. It comes first as energy, light, a presence that pulses my consciousness with some kind of transmission. I feel into the quality of that presence, letting it reveal itself.

Sometimes it emerges as a deep, velvety black presence that is utterly silent, a primordial "is-ness." Sometimes it emerges as a luminous golden light that stretches into infinity with no break or limit anywhere. Sometimes it is like an ocean of clean, crisp, clear awareness. Sometimes it is a point of scintillating light. Sometimes it is as if everything everywhere is an eye of the Divine, seeing and knowing itself. Sometimes it is a felt sense of "heart" that is both Absolute presence and infinite love. Sometimes it feels as if a thousand angels have exploded within the space. Sometimes bodhisattvas and *dakinis* (female deities) fill the horizon of my inner landscape. Sometimes different colors of light pervade and open into a particular body of wisdom. Sometimes not. The more I do not limit the possibilities with my mind, the more free and fluid everything becomes and the more I am taught from within.

OPENING TO THE GREAT RAYS IS NATURAL

The more we relax and adjust to experiencing our boundless nature, the more the miraculous feels not only possible but utterly natural.

You might bump into your boundless true nature on a walk in nature, especially if you are alone and not following your thoughts. You might slip into a felt sense that everything you see is love: the earth, the plants, the creatures, the sky, the sunlight—all alive with luminous loving goodness. This is a powerful and important realization because it is so fulfilling, helping you receive, trust, be happy, and be at peace with life.

You might taste your boundless true nature in silent meditation as a feeling of emptiness or infinite spaciousness. Quite the opposite to your ego fears of it being empty in a deficient, lonely way, it might feel like a vast, clear space, or it might be, as Vajrayana Buddhists call it, "bliss-filled emptiness." This usually helps us feel very light, open, and pure.

You can experience your boundless nature as awake awareness. Not only are you mindful of your inner experience but there is a sense of stepping way back—as a witness of all your experiences. You might feel a transparent allowing of everything, vast like the sky. (We will explore this more specifically in the next chapter.)

You can experience your boundless nature as pure Shakti, the creative intelligence that animates every living thing, including every process in your body and brain, or as pure presence. Longchenpa's treasury of the Dharmadhatu describes our unified field of perception as a "Buddhafield," saying, "The spaciousness pervades everything, joining outside and inside: it has no boundaries, top or bottom, and is beyond direction. As pure presence, it is clear like the sky, nonspacial, nondual. As the vast matrix itself, it is beyond pulsating thought and image."[3]

It is possible to be fully in your body in relative time and space but not bound by local awareness—rather, to see as God sees, to hear as God hears, to look upon all things from unity, with love and wonder.

BEWARE SUBTLE APPROPRIATION

As the curtains of your consciousness open to reveal boundless depths and possibilities, it is important to be on the lookout for the trap of appropriating expanded states to build a juicier, more spiritually expanded ego. What most helps prevent this is remembering that the hallmark of authentic nondual experience is the absence of any grandiosity or narcissism. Arrogance is not possible unless there is a "self" taking personal credit for the spiritual state, thinking it is the do-er, the special one.

We all must keep an eye out for our familiar ego identity reconstellating around refined states we begin to taste. This is yet another reason why it is so important to seek the support of others on the path, to discriminate between genuine openings and subtle bypasses. We must see and forgive our ego tendencies for appropriation, just not feed them.

Another common trap is trying to chase after the spiritual high or trying to cling to expanded states. This is very understandable given how free, how expansive, how beautiful boundless love, awake awareness, pure presence, creative intelligence, and Absolute being are. However, the second any clinging happens, you have looped back into the "me" trying to hold on to the "state." You are back in duality, grasping now for an enlightened condition. It is more helpful instead to put your focus on asking, "What wisdom does this bring? What does this reveal about what really is, how to truly live?"

The point is not having bigger and better spiritual orgasms but being intimate with reality and living that wisdom.

ACCEPTING OUR SHARED IDENTITY

The more intimate you become with your boundless depths, the more you discover that there is no "your" true nature and "my" true nature. While we manifest in miraculous diversity in distinct locations as human beings, animals, plants, and rocks, the fabric of our being is one. What is the consequence of this? *A Course in Miracles* invites us to accept, "I am one Self, united in my Creator; one with all aspects of Creation, and limitless in power and in peace."[4]

Once we have begun to taste our unity, the work then is on *accepting it as your inner platform* so it becomes the new normal. The more you accept the unity from which your individual expression takes shape, the less bound you are by the seemingly fixed laws of the world. You discover a limitless potential for peace, despite the mounting evidence for the lack of it, and unending power to live and express the beauty of what you are. It is not ego power to exert our will simply to obtain more status, money, and things but the power to receive subtle Grace, abide more substantially in reality, and let heavenly realms radiate through us into this world. Surely this is why we are all truly here.

PRACTICAL IMPORTANCE OF BOUNDLESS ABIDING

You might be asking, "Why is opening out to the farthest shores in consciousness so important? What practical good does it really bring to our lives? How useful is it for our troubled world?" Not only does getting to know your deeper nature resolve your inner conflicts and limitations at the root but the unified condition also produces a deeper humanity. When you know that everything you encounter is part of yourself and part of God, you cannot help but feel a deep reverence toward it.

This lends itself to naturally valuing everyone and treating them kindly, as if everyone is your Beloved. When you know that you are not separate from all the animals, trees, and plants, you naturally start to care for other beings and for our environment. This lends itself to wanting to do your part in stewarding the Earth. Your thinking, your decision-making process, and even your day-to-day actions take on more heart. You begin to see that what Ramana called "heart" is not just limited to the cavity in your chest that contains your feelings but a heart-full-ness that can permeate your thinking, your body, and all of your relationships and actions.

GRACE CENTERED IN THE NOW

All of these expanded possibilities are only ever available in the now and possible only when your ego is relaxed, not chasing after anything, not rejecting anything.

When the flow of the internal chatter in the mind quiets down, inner silence frees up energy formerly bound in ego defenses, emotive spasms, fantasies, and fears. Ego centeredness gives way to Grace centeredness, blissfully refining your consciousness. You finally move past the binding impact of the past and enter not just the present moment but the eternal presence.

The more you learn to abide in your boundless nature, the more it continues to dissolve anything fixed and dense. This inevitably begins affecting your linear sense of time and space as well. You slip into the eternal now—a state of Grace where you are simultaneously right here, in your body in a particular location on the planet but not bound by form or location. You may begin to experience and sense other times, other spaces, and even other beings as here, like holographic layers simultaneously present in your own experience.

More than two centuries ago, the great poet William Blake wrote, "To see a World in a Grain of Sand / And a Heaven in a Wild Flower, / Hold Infinity in the palm of your hand / And Eternity in an hour."[5] A. H. Almaas describes this possibility as "unilocal" experience. It is where nonduality gains a holographic quality, with endless possibilities that can contain wisdom from other incarnations and other times experienced as simultaneously here. Yet you cannot chase after this. Grace opens this possibility when you are ready.

What most helps in gaining a foothold in your boundless true nature is continuing to bring attention back to your immediate direct experience. Even though you are not contained by the borders of your body, surprisingly, the greatest ally often is the simplicity of just sensing body sensations in the here and now. This helps you unhook from the tendency to think about your experience and just be here, soft and open—spontaneously available for fresh Grace to emerge. Now that you have learned to practice ego relaxation through the more difficult challenges of fear, control, judgment, pride, anger, and your familiar identity, it is time to let ego relaxation usher you into deeper direct experience of your luminous being. The following meditation is a contemplative practice inspired by one that my friend Richard Steward shared with me.

MEDITATION Abiding in Boundless Nature

This meditation is best done when you have some time and space and ideally in the wake of whatever openings might have taken place from your practice of unwinding your core ego identity. This can even become a regular springboard for silent sitting practice.

Sit in your sacred space where you will not be disturbed. Close your eyes and sink into stillness. Let each inhale welcome you more deeply into the immediacy of the here and now. Sense your body on the chair, cushion, or mat. Sense the ground under you, the cool air arriving into your nostrils. Let each exhale invite a melting, be it of body tension, the following of thought, or the need to chase after anything particular.

Feel the natural rise and fall of your breath support you to just be here, as you are, with nothing you need to get, fix, or do and nothing to seek for or push away from. If the mind gets busy, just come back to sensing the immediacy of your body and breath. Stay with this basic ego relaxation practice until you feel sufficiently settled. Let the following prompts invite you to explore your inner terrain afresh. If you feel any mental "trying" when you answer a question, just return to sensing your body and breath.

1. Without relying on memory and using only your immediate direct experience, do you have a name?

2. Without relying on memory and using only your immediate direct experience, do you have an age?

3. Without relying on memory and using only your immediate direct experience, do you have a gender?

4. Without relying on memory and using only your immediate direct experience, do you have a shape?

5. Without relying on memory and using only your immediate direct experience, do you have a boundary?

6. Without relying on memory and using only your immediate direct experience, are you complete?

7. What is here now? Stretch into whatever is here . . . perhaps a state, silence, spaciousness, certain qualities, timelessness.

8. Does anything need to be added? Does anything need to be taken away?

9. Is there any problem to solve?

10. Who notices all this?

Whatever unfolds, just soften, open, allow, and abide in your deeper nature, which is naturally peaceful. When it feels natural to return to the ordinary realm, do not think of "leaving" the expanded state to come back into the regular world. Rather, let the ordinary world come to you. Perhaps take some deeper breaths and wiggle your fingers and toes, letting your body get used to a more expanded interior. As your eyes slowly open, see if you can avoid "grasping" with your eyes and instead let light, form, and color come to you. See if you can let sounds come to you. See what movement of your body wants to happen, and let what is natural unfold. Each time you practice transitioning from formal meditation, it can be turned into a beautiful practice of learning to abide, while including the regular three-dimensional reality. ~

INQUIRY **Boundless Being, Boundless Wisdom**

Holistic inquiry is phenomenally powerful for illuminating and then dissolving dense boulders of consciousness, but it does not stop there. These three questions invite you to journey to your boundless shores. This is best practiced with a friend offering you the questions, but if that is not possible, put a timer on for fifteen minutes and journal or meditate into them.

1. *What's it like in body, heart, and mind when you experience being boundless?*

2. *How does the world appear?*

3. *What wisdom is revealed?*

Repeat this sequence a number of times. ~

Ultimately, as you practice ego relaxation in and through everything you find inside, the transforming power of Grace refines all that was once fixed, bound, or dense. You return to the fluid freedom of your original true nature, which has no beginning and no end point. Not only do you feel more alive and more fully present but you are also delighted by the simplest of things. When you look around within and without, everything becomes delightful, playful, miraculous. Better still, I have yet to find an end point to the possibility of this waterfall that we are. When your consciousness is no longer bumping up against such big boulders, there is a powerful flow to your way of being that not only brings the life-giving noble qualities online for your personal freedom but also allows this Grace to flow deeper into our world.

PART IV

LIVING THE EMBODIMENT OF GRACE

The person who is in tune with the universe
Becomes like a radio receiver
Through which the Voice of the universe
Is transmitted.

HAZRAT INAYAT KHAN,
The Sufi Message of Hazrat Inayat Khan: Volume 1; The Inner Life

All that we have discovered in our journey so far provides an inner platform for the miraculous. Recognizing that you exist within the ground of Grace makes it truly possible to let the density of your ego's fear, control, and judgment melt. Entering into a receptive state of Grace awakens you to the shower of subtle blessings that are always available to nourish, refine, and uplift your consciousness. Yielding to the living presence beyond your familiar identity dissolves the forces that keep you unnecessarily bound. Each dimension of Grace emerges not in a linear progression but more like a holographic unfolding of your true nature.

Consider the possibility that your body, mind, heart, and every part of your human vessel is much more than it seems. What if you were originally designed to be a Grace-delivery device? A human fountain from which the living waters not only recirculate all the qualities of your boundless nature but overflow to spiritually hydrate our world?

The whole point of spiritual endeavor is not just for some of us to have a happier time of things but for there to be way more spiritually mature, grounded, wise, loving human beings in every country, in every boardroom, in every home.

The fourth dimension of Grace asks you to continue yielding to *the* truth, *the* way, *the* plan. This means continuing to surrender anything that binds your precious life force to self-centered patterns and behaviors. A human fountain stands at the center point, in stillness, with arms outstretched, nectars overflowing. It does not demand that anyone come and drink, it does not require any praise, and it is not perturbed by criticism. The living fountain offers generously to all, for such is the nature of you and I when we know in whom we abide.

The next four chapters invite you to stabilize and embody your realization. Take a deeper seat with equanimity so you can stride deeper into our world, which surely needs more of us to be graceful. Discover the possibilities for more potent, inspired action in daily life. Befriend rather than transcend your animal humanity. More than anything, *be* the presence of love here on Earth. In these times, every one of us is needed now.

13 CULTIVATING EQUANIMITY IN UNCERTAIN TIMES

If you don't realize the source,
you stumble in confusion and sorrow.
When you realize where you come from,
you naturally become tolerant,
disinterested, amused,
kind-hearted as a grandmother,
dignified as a king.

LAO TZU, ***Tao Te Ching*** **(translated by Stephen Mitchell)**

Once you begin to taste the freedom of your true nature and are no longer bound by your ego identifications, your way of being can become significantly more graceful. Just as a tiny jasmine blossom can powerfully uplift a whole room with its heavenly scent, you can go about your responsibilities with your family, colleagues, and community while radiating peace and clarity. The virtue of equanimity helps you take a noble seat inside from which you become more spiritually elegant. It helps you stabilize in that which is never rocked, even though the ground beneath your feet may be quaking. Cultivating equanimity increases your capacity to respond wisely to the changing landscape of life.

FIRST, RELAX YOUR REACTIVITY

In recent years, more people have come to me seeking support not just in navigating their personal spiritual challenges but in learning how to grapple honestly with their concerns about the state of our world. I do not claim to have the answer, but I do have great faith in the power of holistic inquiry to access the wisdom we each need to bring forth our best. What often blights the way is our ego's tendency to launch into problem-solving from within a consciousness of polarization. Before you can wisely respond, first you must relax your ego's effort to troubleshoot from its inevitably limited understanding. Without first relaxing your reactivity, being in the world from a consciousness beyond it is impossible.

Even when you know that taking a moment to practice ego relaxation rather than just running into action from reaction is sage advice, it can trigger fierce resistance. You would not be alone in insisting that the problems you perceive *must* be fixed before any peace or equanimity is possible. This is a variation of the ego demand we discussed in chapter 9 on forgiveness: "If this changes, I can be at peace." Feeding this insistence will only bind your precious resources. Better to engage the virtues of trust, patience, humility, sincerity, and forgiveness to serve you in meeting everything with an open, loving heart. Then the clarity about what to do or not do can find you.

Sometimes you cannot help but get triggered into reactivity, especially in the areas that matter most to you: your intimate relationships, family, career, or health. Equanimity helps you to accept your humanity and forgive your attachments to a particular outcome. Then it is possible to be graceful even when a wave of anger arises. Rather than judging, projecting, or blaming, with equanimity you just meet whatever comes up as information, energy, or heat so it can burn the false down to something more essential.

MEETING CHALLENGING TIMES WITH SPIRITUAL MATURITY

In these complex, uncertain times across the globe, we need spiritual practice more than ever, not just to give us respite from the intensity but also to grow deeper and broader roots inside, as a great tree does, so we may be more flexible with the winds of change. There is a great need for more of us to stabilize our realization, not just for our own peace of mind but so our way of being provides spiritual shelter for others.

It is not easy to stabilize in equanimity when confronted by the news of yet another painful explosion of hatred, extremism, racism, or violence, not to mention the increasing natural disasters arising from climate change. It is deeply disappointing to behold leaders behaving disgracefully and corporate greed remaining unchecked. The way of Grace does not grasp for a spiritual platitude to push past the challenges of our times that do not have easy answers. While you might want to be selective about the quality and quantity of the media you engage in, at the same time you will not mature spiritually by living in a news-free bubble or by getting hysterical or dissipating your precious energy by railing against what is.

Living gracefully means turning everything into the path of awakening. This can include practicing ego relaxation while taking in the news. Equanimity invites you to not judge the judgment or hate the hateful and to forgive yourself when you slip into polarization anyway. Marianne Williamson invites us to think of the news as humanity's prayer list. When you take in a news report from the awareness that you are not separate from everyone and everything, natural compassion arises for "our" collective ignorance and suffering.

Living gracefully amidst challenging times calls us into a new prayer:

> May I stabilize in the infinite Source,
> open my heart to all that arises,
> and grow into a deeper, wiser,
> more responsive human being.

Living into such a prayer asks you to embrace all that is arising, within and without, as part of the full mandala of your life.

ACCEPTING IMPERMANENCE IN THE DIVINE CLASSROOM

It is easier to take the noble seat in equanimity when you consider this world will always be a world of impermanence. All wisdom traditions understand that all things that appear will also disappear. However, each path has its own cosmology offering a distinct perspective on what reality is, what the world is for, and what the ultimate goal is for humanity. Seen through a Buddhist or Vedantic cosmology, the physical world is seen as *maya*, "illusion," or *leela*, "divine play." Therefore, the teachings and practices tend to have a more transcendental emphasis, focusing on elevating consciousness. On the opposite end of the spectrum is Judaism, where the world is seen as unquestionably real and part of God's creation, a view shared by the other Abrahamic traditions, Christianity and Islam. The Hebrew precept of *tikum olam* charges human beings with the task of healing what is broken in the world. While these cosmologies differ vastly, every tradition has produced some truly luminous, exceptional human beings who have brought great benefit to our world. This shows there is value and wisdom in all views.

I find it helpful to view this world as a divine classroom, a place of learning and evolution. Mysteriously, we all seem to be working through a highly personalized version of essentially the same curriculum. We all are charged with waking up out of ego fear, separation, pride, deception, closure, anger, and hate. We are all asked to evolve beyond self-centeredness, to serve one another somehow by embodying our divine qualities of love, truth, compassion, beauty, and peace.

The precise set of circumstances you most need to become more graceful might look very different from those of your best friend. Embrace the precise gifts and challenges contained in the particular curriculum called your life, and the false will inevitably be sloughed off to reveal more of the inner jewel.

INCLUDE YOUR RELATIVE AND ABSOLUTE EXPERIENCE

The nondual cosmology of Kashmir Shaivism, or Trika yoga, helps us understand that the absolute depths of our unchanging nature and the relative level of our changing experience are not, fundamentally, two separate things but part of one stream of being. This view is echoed in Taoism and Tibetan Buddhism. When we do not reject either dimension, everything is revealed as divine, even when it may be manifesting into a difficult form. Mother Teresa embodied this understanding in the way she described the lepers she cared for in India as "Christ, in all of His distressing disguises."

This integrated nondual view helps us see that even the crude, dense, difficult distortions of ego—ours and those of our politicians—are still fundamentally God, just God caught up in some dense suffering and ignorant of itself. Just as the fundamental substance of a hard chunk of ice is still water, the parts of ourselves and others that are opaque, frozen in fixation, and fixed in ignorant patterns are still God . . . although clearly not in its free and fluid condition. But they can become so.

Walking this world while understanding that everything is divine does not ask you to deny difficulties. Living gracefully is not wafting above the muck and mess in a transcendent pastel vapor. However, remembering that everything is a display in the one fabric protects you from getting lost in the appearances and losing your inner seat and thus neutering your graceful response. Equanimity blossoms when you allow all things to be exactly the way they are.

ABIDE IN WITNESSING AWARENESS

Hindu sage and author of *Autobiography of a Yogi*, Paramahansa Yogananda, once asked the luminous feminine mystic Sri Anandamayi Ma to tell him something of her life. She responded, "There is little to tell. My consciousness has never fully associated itself with this temporary body. Before I came on this earth, 'I was the same.' I grew into womanhood but still 'I was the same.' When the family into which I had been born made arrangements to have this body married, 'I was the same.' And father, in front of you now, 'I am the same.' Even afterwards, though the dance of creation changes around me in the hall of eternity, 'I shall be the same.'"[1]

The transcendent depth of us all is timeless, formless, changeless, infinite spirit. It is pristine, immune to any harm, and it does not die. Finding your footing in this depth provides a powerful platform to be at peace, independent of the troubles in our world and the challenges you might be facing personally. While it seems esoteric, this understanding has the power to help you find true ground in those moments when everything you thought was solid is revealed to be unreliable. Let us take a few minutes to access this depth of your nature with the following reflection exercise. It is more natural and accessible than you might think.

REFLECTION **Witnessing Awareness**

Feel into the awareness of being here, where you are, holding this book and taking in these words.

Lean into the field of your awareness—the consciousness that is looking out of your eyes but is not defined by a sense of physical location.

It might feel as if you are taking a step back inside to the "I" that has been there always, the witness that has no age and is not defined by any of your experiences.

See if you can become aware of the awareness of the room and everything and everyone in the room.

Instead of relating to all the "things" as concrete objects, separate from you, relax into the awareness that is aware of everything but not defined by it. Stretch into that space. It might feel like you *are* the space pervading everything.

Notice that the awareness has no fixed ending or beginning. It just *is*. You just *are*.

In this witnessing awareness, you are naturally peaceful, naturally accepting of everything, and not attached to particulars. ~

Abiding in this depth has helped me to be graceful within some extremely challenging situations in my personal journey, and it can be helpful for yours too. However, a common fear you might encounter as you find your footing in witnessing awareness is the fear that you will become too detached and lose your heart. Abiding in witnessing awareness brings a quality of dispassion, or neutrality. You might notice feeling that you are not so invested in what happens or does not happen. This is because your attachment to particular outcomes and thought streams starts falling away. It is the beginning of your heart becoming more objective and thus less emotionally reactive.

How can you discriminate whether this is a subtle dissociative defense or authentic detachment? Truth will always leave you feeling clear, present, and open. While it can lay a boundary, it will never produce hardness or closure. Since witnessing awareness is not attached to thoughts, emotions, experiences, perceptions, roles, or sensations, it has no problem with opening to all that arises.

ALLOW YOUR CHANGING CONTENT

Mysteriously, our unchanging essence is alive and constantly changing in content. On the relative level, we are unique human beings who experience all kinds of internal weather. Our bodies grow, develop, fluctuate in weight and vitality, age, and eventually die. Our understanding, moods, and viewpoints change. Our world is constantly unfolding, sometimes taking very unexpected turns. No amount of spiritual practice will halt this. It is not supposed to. Equanimity accepts the fact of this undulation, both within our Self and in the environment in which we move and have our life.

You and I learned how to be in this world and function from the dual perspective of a separate "me" who is fundamentally insecure and thus at the mercy of all of this change. This is why even after experiencing your boundless nature (as you likely have in the course of reading this book), it usually takes a lot longer to actually live your life from this depth of being.

Relating to your changing relative experience as "content" supports you to remain in the noble seat while opening to the nuances and layers of your experience, both what appears as inner and outer. If you explore your inner terrain thoroughly, there will often be layers of belief or *perception*, certain feelings or *tones*, various *body sensations* (which can range from tingling, hot, and cold to shimmering energies), a *view on reality*, and sometimes an *identity* to whom this all belongs. But the deeper you go, the more "self" disappears. By practicing ego relaxation—learning to just be here and do nothing—your inner content refines, granting exponential access to the subtle depths, the boundless qualities that we touched upon in the previous chapter.

If you are *only* in touch with your relative content and do not have access to witnessing awareness, you will get rocked around a great deal. You will insist that peace is only possible when your circumstances are pleasing, your children are happy, your preferred political party is in power, or you have finally lost those extra pounds. You will take your thoughts and emotions to be facts rather than responses to limited perceptions. This leads you to get lost in the particulars, whether that be what you experience inwardly or what you perceive in your environment.

Yet dismissing your relative humanity and focusing on the transcendent only makes you vulnerable to the dangers of bypassing. Some people start to view their relative experience as illusory, not worth their attention, something to be dismissed. I feel that this is an expression of the masculine-dominant focus that has pervaded spiritual teachings for too many years and has valued transcendence over immanence. Whether you are in a male or a female body, both dimensions of our nature are equally God—and thus equally important.

Embracing both the unchanging awareness and your very human relative experience helps you meet the inevitable fluctuations of life—the family challenges, an aging body, financial ups and downs, joyful celebrations, and the uncertainty in the world—in the spirit of unconditional allowing. Just as the atmosphere allows space for both trees and pollution, equanimity helps you meet absolutely everything in the spirit of "this too."

SIT DEEPER *IN*, *BACK*, AND *WIDE* WITHIN

Energetically, equanimity feels like being deeper *in* your essential being. You are not taken by the appearances of what seems to be happening in the environment and insisting it needs to change. Rather, you are more settled internally, aware of your inner core, receiving the ground not just of this Earth but the ground of Grace. Simultaneously, the space above your crown is open and receptive to subtle dimensions of light and presence. You feel a kind of vertical spaciousness, centered depth, and fluidity.

Equanimity also feels like being deeper *back* inside. Your energy is not so externally oriented, not reaching outward for mirroring or security from the environment. Rather, your energy is back and settled, in contact with your belly, receiving the nourishment of your breath and your inner pulse.

Equanimity also has a sense of *width*. Your consciousness feels much wider than your physical body, as if you were backing into infinite perspective, space, and nonlocal awareness. You feel a spontaneous availability to qualities, capacities, and intelligence that you did not create or earn. You feel your human vehicle as a divine vessel. You feel connected inside to what's true, and thus your consciousness grows increasingly calm and clear.

Equanimity is a graceful, mature state in which you are relaxed and in touch with the "both-and" nature of things. Now that you have had a taste of being so much more than your personality, it is time to explore how to be with all the content unfolding within and all the things appearing to unfold "outside." The following inquiry sequence is somewhat advanced, so go slowly and be patient.

INQUIRY **The Grace of Equanimity**

This sequence of questions is designed to help you journey through the layers of your direct experience. It does not matter whether your starting experience is pleasing or difficult. With practice, you will discover that engaging in this when you are triggered is incredibly supportive. You might find that you have easier access to some layers than others. This reveals where you are most attached—body, emotions, thoughts. You will grow the most if you dive deeper into the layers you have the *least access to* and tend to skim over. Your goal here is not problem-solving, but deeper wisdom. You will not arrive by thinking but by entering into the dimensions of your experience.

1. *What is unfolding in the content of your experience?*
   Notice the layers without telling a story about them; just open, soften, and allow the layers of thought, feeling, sensation, view, identity, and space. Dive deep.

- What thoughts or perceptions are here?
- What feelings and emotions are here?
- What body sensations do you notice? (Such as heat, energy, tingling, tightness, openness, etc.)
- What is your "view" on reality? (For example, "Reality is loving," "It's a crazy, scary world," etc.)
- Whom does this experience belong to? (For example, a five-year-old, your ancestors, your culture or gender, no self, etc.)
- What else is here—space, subtle qualities, insights?

Take at least fifteen minutes to explore these layers in detail, perhaps doing another round beginning with the first question in this sequence, until you feel deeply in touch with yourself, fluid, and open.

When you can meet the layers without grasping or rejecting, inevitably your experience will start to refine and become more spacious. Then you can start to explore the *space your experience is happening within.* If you can relax trying to get yourself into any particular state or change or fix your content and instead just stretch out more deeply inside, you will begin to bump into the pure awareness that always *is.*

This witnessing awareness is not just a state, not just a dimension of your boundless nature. It is the *medium of all your experiences.* This can often feel like being a still lake that mirrors the sky or like a transparent liquid.

The next question invites you to notice how it is if you allow both the content of your experience—inner and outer—*and* notice the awareness witnessing it, not by attaching to one or the other, but allowing both-and. Question 3 invites you to explore how the world appears from this vantage point. Let your consciousness take flight.

2. *What's it like if you allow both the content of your experience and the awareness that is witnessing it?*

3. *How does the world appear from here?*

Journey with questions 2 and 3 for fifteen minutes or more. ~

When you relax with the totality of your experience, it becomes more apparent that your personal, limited, and even egoic experience is, at its depth, infinitely miraculous. Really, yours is a divine basement always. Recognizing this enables you to harness absolutely everything into a gateway for deeper wisdom—the beauty and the horror and everything in between. Resting in the unchanging, you can be more fully here and more fully human. The Grace of equanimity can ripple its peace and perspective through your body, heart, and mind, making you beautifully responsive and ripe with wisdom to bless our world.

14 INSPIRED ACTION

Whatever I do, the responsibility is mine,
but like one who plants an orchard,
what comes of what I do, the fruit,
will be for others.

I offer the actions of this life
to the God within,
and wherever I go, the way is blessed.

LALLA, *Naked Song* (translated by Coleman Barks)

Cultivating equanimity gives you a deeper and broader seat inside so you can greet the inevitable ups and downs of life from the vantage point of witnessing awareness. Just as the sky allows for all kinds of weather, you can allow all emotions, states, and experiences to unfold without getting swept away by them. From this strong inner foundation, you can turn your attention toward being of benefit to our world. How can your everyday actions become more potent, precise, effortless, and wise?

LET DOING HAPPEN FROM BEING

Even when you have come to see that you are not ultimately the do-er, that you are being lived and breathed by the same power and majesty that creates the mountains, it is a significant adjustment to let your moment-to-moment actions emerge from this foundation. Our ego mind struggles to reconcile doing with being, superficially confusing ego relaxation with behaving like a couch potato. While awakening into a state of Grace can happen in a split second, actualizing the wisdom all the way through the way you relate, think, and act is a much longer, nuanced process.

This is because you and I learned how to do everything—from cooking breakfast and having a conversation to complex tasks like managing finances—from the perspective of a separate "me." All too often, we automatically revert back to the familiar habits of ego effort to get through the trials of any given day. What does it take to unlearn the neural pathways of separation? How can we find a more elegant way of going about our business?

Just as an overdeveloped muscle will dominate the way your body moves unless you deliberately strengthen other balancing muscles, embodying Grace amidst the daily grind requires commitment. First, see where you are picking up the old tension patterns. Where do you muscle through?

You will always know when your ego is driving your actions because it will feel stressful. Your body contracts, your breath shallows, and your mind spins into overwhelm trying to figure it all out. You believe you have to create the support, that you have make it happen. You feel pressure, and you likely pressure others. Life is not fun when you are not in the flow.

TAKE EGO RELAXATION BREAKS

The wisest thing you can do when you realize you are acting from the limited consciousness of your ego is to just stop and have a few ego relaxation minutes. In a moment of stress, you will likely encounter strong resistance to this suggestion, thinking you don't have time. I dare you to set a personal reminder for a handful of three-minute ego relaxation breaks to punctuate your working day. Then, actually stop and allow Grace to reset you. Perhaps lie on the floor and take some deep breaths: Just be nothing, do nothing, get nothing, become nothing, seek for nothing, relinquish nothing. Be as you are. Rest in God. (You can even download a recording of a free guided reset, and many other tools, from the sanctuary within my website at mirandamacpherson.com.)

Then return to the task at hand, but more slowly, remembering that the same primordial intelligence that causes all things to exist knows precisely how to tackle this task with impeccable competency. As *A Course in Miracles* points out, "Who would attempt to fly with the tiny wings of a sparrow when the mighty power of an eagle has been given him?"[1]

Graceful action arises out of your commitment to remain intimate with the cause of your being and then to let this move you into action. Sensing your feet on the floor, your body held by the chair, and the breath naturally rising and falling supports greater depth of presence as you respond to emails, drive the kids to school, or prepare for an important presentation.

Recognizing you are always in an infinite ground as well as an infinite shower of Grace, you naturally grow more responsive. The wisdom needed to be skillful with every task is present. You begin to sit deeper in, back, and wide within your noble seat. You become more surrendered to flow with what's true, what makes the best sense, and what seems to be *the* plan for the day. Your ordinary functioning becomes cleaner, less self-centered, and way more efficient.

EGO RELAXATION LIBERATES YOUR GIFTS

We all naturally want to manifest our full potential in life, to embody who we really are. Paradoxically, it is when you let go of trying to be special, to make your mark on the world, to *prove* something, or to *get* something that luminous qualities fly forward just as light pours through a clean windowpane. In the same way that a windowpane does not claim ownership of the light that pours through it, remembering the source of your gifts protects them from being co-opted to build a more successful brand of ego. When talents, capacities, and realizations come together, manifesting your full potential is not about "you" anymore. Rather, your joy, talent, or skill just expresses in some way that uplifts or serves.

One summer evening while visiting New York City, my husband and I visited a tiny crowded bar in the West Village where the jazz virtuoso Mike Stern was playing. Sandwiched between a drummer and bass player, he had just walked downstairs with wet hair, fresh from the shower of his apartment above. A broad smile radiated from his open face, as nimble hands on the guitar birthed ecstatic melodies with the fluidity of a sonic waterfall. Naturally and completely giving his musical gift, without any shred of "look at me." Everyone in the bar received the blessing. It was as pure as anything you might find in any church or temple.

I recently learned that Mike tripped on the street outside that bar, sustaining devastating injuries to his guitar-playing arms and hands. After a lengthy rehab, he continues to perform with that same broad smile and graceful countenance, albeit with a guitar pic taped to his immobilized hand. His latest album is called *Trip!* Such is the unstoppable offering of a human fountain.

SURRENDERING TO DEEPER INTELLIGENCE

How can your talents and noble qualities be freed from self-centeredness to blossom in ways that serve our world? As we have seen, Grace always asks for some kind of surrender. For inspired action, this means surrendering the tendency to lead with the mind. Just as your body finds natural, authentic movement by surrendering to the music, in yielding to a primordial pulse, you discover your own nature is part of Divine Intelligence itself.

One of the greatest concerns I hear from sincere aspirants is that such surrender will render us into a useless, jellylike blob on the floor, unable to function effectively as a parent, a partner, or a professional in the world—that if we completely let go of needing to prove ourselves worthy, good enough, or lovable, we would not be motivated to do anything. Implied in these fears is mistrust in our own basic goodness, mistrust that Grace itself knows what it is doing, and mistrust that we could be moved into action from inspiration.

These same hidden concerns held me back for years. In the two years prior to the seismic shift in Ramana's cave, I was aware of a subtle resistance in my meditation practice. In the deep silence, it felt as if "I" was starting to disappear. At first this was exquisitely peaceful, but then "I" would pop back up, hesitant to fully trust the gravitational lure of the void lest I become unable to move, eat, or speak, let alone hold a spiritual organization together. By Grace that day in the cave, disappearing happened anyway. I am delighted to report that surrendering did not hamper my capacity to function. It powerfully enhanced it. Talents and capacities I did not know existed began to reveal themselves. Functioning became much more direct. As Ralph Waldo Emerson said in one of his essays on spiritual laws back in 1842, "Let us take our bloated nothingness out of the path of the divine circuits."[2]

In the years that followed, I learned that the more I surrendered my plan for *the* plan, the more powerfully everything found its synchronistic flow. It helped that the challenges of my personal situation at the time were way beyond my personality's capacity to navigate. There was little choice but to give up leading from the mind in everyday life. Since discovering that who I had taken myself to be was really a network of limited self-images anyway, learning to make no decisions from my "self" made good practical sense.

ASKING AND LISTENING FOR EVERY ACTION

I had been listening to the still small voice in the silence of morning meditation since my early twenties. While I would often tap into a stream of clarity that would pour out onto the page of my journal, much of the time I did not know how to live its wisdom. Despite the luminosity my meditation would reveal, it was humbling how often I would just muscle through my to-do list in that clunky old way.

After the cave awakening, the sense of "me" asking a Supreme Being for guidance felt redundant. Settling into the landscape beyond subject-object, asking morphed into these questions: "What wants to be received? Known? Released? Done?" In recent years, it has become even simpler, just praying: "What's needed now?" and listening to what comes.

I have trained myself to lean into these three words before making any decision. At first, it was helpful to ask for everyday things that did not seem to matter much, like, "What does the body want for lunch today?" When my GPS provides three travel routes to get to the same destination, I ask, "What's the smoothest journey?" When there are many important deadlines to meet, I ask, "What's the priority?" Frankly, writing this book and all of the teachings and practices emerged out of this question. It is an ongoing moment-to-moment practice that I find very supportive in embodying Grace in the ordinariness of life.

Opening the tap of inspiration requires you to be quiet, allow space, and continue to abide in the unified, natural condition where you are already at one with Divine Intelligence, creativity, power, and peace. The deeper you rest in God, the less you even need specific questions. There is no limit to what can come online if you rest empty and listen.

LIVING IN SPIRITUAL OBEDIENCE

One of the most extraordinary embodiments of this "spiritual obedience" I know was the late Eileen Caddy, one of the three founders of the Findhorn Foundation in Scotland. Eileen was devoted to living the quintessential invitation to "Be still and know I am God." For her, that meant regular periods of silent meditation and listening to what she called the "voice of God," which would pour out onto the page of her journal.

The specific vision and execution for the extraordinary intentional community that became Findhorn was birthed out of Eileen's inner listening. Each day, her husband, Peter, would take those morning pages as the "orders" for action. A former air force commander and deeply masculine being, Peter embodied the principle that "work is love in action." He had a great talent for galvanizing everyone into high gear. Dorothy Maclean joined the Caddys with her gift of attuning to and cooperating with the spirit of nature. Together, they formed a mighty collaboration that birthed a new possibility for spirituality, community, and ecology.

I had the great privilege of spending time with Eileen in the final eighteen months of her life, when she was physically very frail but inwardly luminous as ever. She told me of the early years, when she was living in a tiny Airstream trailer parked on the sand dunes. During the brutal Scottish winters, her husband would be away working for long periods, leaving Eileen to care for two boisterous boys in the middle of nowhere. Waking at 4:00 a.m., Eileen would take her journal to the only private place she had—the concrete shower block.

There she would light a candle and sit huddled in blankets in the dark of the early morning silence, listening. The transmissions she received have fed thousands of souls across the world.

The meditation below is one I have shared with many students over the years to open up the flow of inspiration.

MEDITATION **Opening to Inner Wisdom**

This practice is best integrated into your existing practice, toward the end of formal meditation. The foundation for inner wisdom always begins with settling into the quiet depth of your being. There is no point asking for guidance from the consciousness of a separate "me" who is grasping for a response. The more you draw into the center point of stillness, with nothing to get, fix, or prove, the more can come online. Everything you could possibly need to live meaningfully is already shimmering. From here, right action finds itself.

1. Sit in your sacred space, with a journal or perhaps drawing materials in front of you.

2. Engage in the basic Melting into Ego Relaxation meditation, or any of the meditation practices that work best to help you settle into the deep quiet, let go, and abide in unity. Stay with this until you feel deeply settled and quiet.

3. In the stillness, drop into the following four questions one at a time. Just like dropping a penny into a still pond, let them ripple through.
   - What wants to be received? (Here, just take in what comes.)
   - What wants to be known? (Here, move to your journal or drawing.)
   - What wants to be released?
   - What wants to be done?

4. Let your hand move across the page without editing, or let drawing happen if that is more natural for you. Do not "think" about what you are writing or whether it makes any sense. Do not try too hard. You may or may not "hear" anything. You may, however, feel as if your consciousness is being permeated with a quality of presence. You might "see" an image unfolding across the screen of your consciousness. Do not grasp, as the response might come later when you are not trying. Whatever comes, remember that what matters most is not necessarily the particulars, but the *wisdom* revealed. Grace will always bring forth what is useful. Often this is surprising, so be open.

5. If there is some specific challenge you are facing in your life, ask: *Regarding (name the situation), what's needed?*

6. Sit a little longer with the wisdom that is revealed. Notice how it feels energetically in the body. How does it affect the heart? See how it naturally moves you into the day.

Do not get attached to hearing a "voice," for inspiration may not take that form for you. Commonly, a response comes as a fresh idea arriving as if out of nowhere or a new possibility presenting itself that had not occurred before. Perhaps long after your meditation, a colleague or friend says something or something you read just "sings" to you in a way that you know is the truth. Most importantly, the true response is always some form of peace. ~

DISCRIMINATING SUBTLE DELUSION FROM TRUTH

Before springing into action, it is important to run whatever you receive through these discriminating gates: "Is the tone fundamentally peaceful and nonharming?" "Does this serve the propagation of truth, love, and compassion?" Anything you receive that has a tone of hatred or judgment or is dehumanizing to anyone is clearly a distortion. Disregard it. Our world does not need any further acting out of hatred in the guise of spirituality.

Be very clear that Truth is never going to inflate your ego into some grandiose fantasy that you, singly, are going to save the world. Everyone can make a positive contribution, but alongside many others as part of a greater whole. True guidance will always bring you back into the deepest alignment with the unified Source. Here, any whiff of ego-aggrandizing disappears, making you deeply humble. Pay more attention to how true guidance helps dissolve inner conflicts, clear up confusions, and usher you toward embodying the noble qualities of a beautiful human being.

The more you get a feel for listening and discriminating, the more you begin to recognize the clean, clear logic of Divine Mind. You begin to see from a unified vision that is always oriented to what serves the whole, what propagates love, peace, and the evolution of our world. Its effect will be beauty. Attuning to this refined logic begins to teach you what is and is not right action.

BEING MOVED TO SERVE

By now it should be clear that ego relaxation means dissolving "I" and "mine" in some way. Realizing there actually is no "other" naturally starts to change what you want to give your time and energy to. Participating in gossip or endless rounds of social media becomes less interesting. Just making more money and buying more stuff feels vacuous. Helping your fellow beings feels meaningful and utterly joyful. The more you taste Grace, the more you naturally feel moved to put your capacities and talents toward what helps or heals in some way. Besides, our world at present could really do with all hands on deck.

The good news is that serving can be simple and plentiful amidst your life as it is. Your talents might not lend themselves to masterminding some philanthropic nonprofit that helps end starvation. It does not have to be grand. The first place to embody inspired action is within the life you have. If you are a mother, how could you be a more beautiful mother to your children? How could you be more present, real, kind, and supportive to your partner? How could you be more fully human with everyone you encounter today? Who in your circle of family, friends, and neighbors could do with a listening ear, a kind hand in some way? If you have enough money to pay your expenses without stress, what project or cause inspires you to donate?

What would be the most enjoyable, natural way to share your experience, love, or expertise? Consider taking one simple action in response to this today. Better still, see how it feels to just do it when no one is looking! Without serving others in some way, whatever you might have realized inwardly does not fully integrate. It is by sharing the fruits that you fully recognize the blessings you have.

EFFORTLESSLY FULFILLING YOUR FUNCTION

When we are not operating out of our ego fixations, lending a helping hand to our fellow beings is effortless. Grounded in the noble seat of equanimity, while letting your heart be opened by devastating impacts of war, wildfire, flooding, and any manner of challenges, it is natural to consider, "How could I help?" There will naturally be some phases of life that are more active than others. You might donate funds, volunteer your time, or at the very least include others in your prayer life. Without this, our spiritual practice runs the risk of becoming a subtly narcissistic endeavor. Let this be very clear: there is no authentic awakening that does not include the awakening of others.

In the mysterious architecture of your life, there will be "assignments" you are given, certain individuals or clusters of people you intuitively know are your flock to tend, or some task you know is yours to fulfill. This will be highly personal for each of us. If you stay receptive, you will notice that the unseen intelligence knows precisely whose gifts and qualities best match one another's. It will present you with invitations to give and receive in ways that grow you deeper, purer, and wiser.

Looking back over my own "career," I never consciously set out to be a spiritual teacher. I just always loved having deep, meaningful conversations with people about what really mattered in life. Every time an inner gate would open, automatically my consciousness would inquire: "How can others experience this liberation also?" Without any real effort on my part, people would ask for help with important grapplings of the soul. I marvel at how everyone who seemed to be "assigned" to me grew my capacities in some important way. It is in engaging with these mysterious assignments that we recognize that giving and receiving really are one.

KEEPING IT CLEAN

In the Bhagavad Gita, the divine guide Krishna counsels the prince Arjuna, who is having a spiritual crisis on the battlefield: "Always perform your duty efficiently and without attachment to the results. By doing work without attachment one attains the Supreme."[3] This sounds noble, but to authentically live it is an enormous invitation. This is why many consider karma yoga—union with God through selfless service—one of the most powerful ways to embody realization. It is by offering yourself fully that you get to see how invested you really are in "me," how attached you are to getting a certain "result."

Inevitably, it is more enjoyable when we lend a hand and it is received well. It is much more challenging when we put the needs of our aging mother before our own, and she is cranky, demanding, and not necessarily appreciating our efforts. Other times, we let it all go and find we are just moved to attend to the needs of others that are genuinely greater than our own. In these pure moments where we evolve beyond self-centeredness, love unfolding in human action is blissful.

Many years ago, I read an interview where the Dalai Lama shared some of his personal spiritual practice. One of the many things he listed was spending one hour a day "purifying his motivation" for all that he does in the world! Even the noble desire to help others can become a subtle costume the ego takes on when no one is looking. Given that we all learn to speak, behave, and act by imitating our elders, it is wise to keep a vigilant and yet forgiving eye out for the reemergence of a "me" who is looking to score some spiritual brownie points for "serving."

A sign that a "self" has appropriated the service is that you feel a sense of sacrifice or pressure, or you get upset when your efforts are not seen or appreciated. Rather than hope this does not happen to you, it is wiser to flush out your hidden ego fantasy right up front, so you can keep on the lookout for the likelihood of it slipping in and taking over. This is what the following inquiry is designed to do.

INQUIRY **Flush Out Your Hidden Fantasy for Service**

Jim Leonard, one of my early teachers in breath work, gave some sage advice when working with the shadow: "Enthusiastically exaggerate it!" This sounds strange, I know, but it works to playfully flush appropriation out into the full light of awareness. I recommend you engage this practice at the outset of any major creative project or impetus to serve. Revisit it often if you start to feel resentful or in sacrifice.

Begin by settling into your quiet space. Consider the way you feel called to serve; perhaps it's a creative project or the impetus to volunteer, donate, or offer yourself.

What does my ego secretly fantasize I can get out of this?
Do not hold back or try to be "spiritual" about it. Just tell the unedited, raw truth.

If that fantasy came true, what do I hope that will do for me?
Again, tell the raw, unedited truth. Notice also how it feels in your body. It will likely feel a bit guttural, instinctual. Let that be.

Who is this "me" really?
Do not presume, but it is likely you will discover a child inside who feels starved for attention, or perhaps a layer of cultural conditioning. Just see.

Now, write this out, and put it on your altar if you have one, as if literally giving it over to the Source. If you have been engaging these practices and inquiries with a trusted friend, tell them about it and agree to talk about it kindly. Additionally, in your next meditation, journey into that heart-cave of Absolute Love that you discovered in chapter 7 and put the fruits of this inquiry on the inner altar of the Absolute to be forgiven and reset. ~

ACTION POWERED BY PRAYER

Ultimately, right action begins from the humble posture of not knowing—not presuming you should know but bowing to the mystery. This soft, surrendered state is always what helps us to be spontaneously receptive to all the states and streams of Grace. From here, we can pray into any sincere question and be moved into right response. You do not have to have "faith" in some supreme deity. You do not have to be religious. There is no wrong and right way to pray. Really, prayer is an offering of your deep heart's desire to be in alignment, to be useful, and to be utilized in the way that is best, most efficient, and elegant.

Who is praying to what exactly? Doesn't prayer pull you back into duality? Whether it feels like you are praying to the intelligence that is your deepest nature or to a Supreme Being really does not matter. Just get on your knees and see what it takes for you to stay there, to live your life in that humble space where your heart intuitively knows that every little word and gaze matters, where what you really want is to love, serve, and remember. Here are some of my most-used prayers. Feel free to make them your own.

- *Take me, use me*. (This helps you remember you are not the do-er.)

- *What's needed now*? (Notice what naturally calls to you.)

- *What is "the way"*? (Notice how it feels to let go of "me" and "my" way.)

- *What is the action that best serves peace*? (Notice that true peace is not necessarily superficial harmony.)

- *If the direction I am moving is not in accordance with the highest truth, please intervene in a way I cannot ignore.* (Just saying a prayer like this is an expression of your deepest intent to be real, sincerely wanting a course correction in case you might be off. Every time I have uttered this prayer, the response has been very dramatic—and thus very clarifying.)

- *Put the thoughts into my mind and the words into my mouth that are most needed, healing, and helpful.* (Use this prayer when sitting with someone who is in a challenging situation and you do not have a clue of what to do or say. This prayer is also fabulous when you're facing relational conflict, and you feel tempted to devolve into accusation, blame, and defense.)

Ultimately, prayer is like a rudder that steers the course, carrying your sincere intention into embodiment as you rest in the receptive condition. Pray often. Pray for everything. Just speak the truth of your heart, not holding anything back. Then listen, not just with your inner ears but with all your senses, to the dynamic intelligence that moves you. It is your best guide for potent, clean action. You can be moved to express, collaborate, create, and serve but without all that flapping around. In these challenging times, our world needs many more of us capable of being fully present in chaotic and difficult circumstances, to help and to heal, to make space for the emergence of new possibilities, and more than ever, to embody true humanity.

15 BEFRIENDING YOUR ANIMAL HUMANITY

This blessing takes one look at you and all it can say is "Holy." Holy hands, holy face, holy feet, holy everything in between. Holy even in pain. Holy even when weary. In brokenness, holy. In shame, holy still. Holy in delight. Holy in distress. Holy when being born. Holy when we lay it down at the hour of our death. So friend, open your eyes (holy eyes). For one moment, see what this blessing sees, this blessing that knows how you have been formed and knit together in wonder and in love. Welcome this blessing that folds its hands in prayer when it meets you: Receive this blessing that wants to kneel in reverence before you—who are temple, sanctuary, home for God in this world.

JAN RICHARDSON, ***Circle of Grace***

When beginning to soar into expanded states, it is tempting to just transcend the body and no longer be bothered by its increasing needs and limitations. Embodying Grace calls for a fresh exploration of our human vessel itself. Our animal humanity, with its hungers for comfort and sensual pleasure, has often been regarded as a difficult beast to be tamed by classical spiritual traditions in both the East and West. Thus we have inherited models of practice that have viewed the body with disregard and sometimes disdain, often encouraging us to push past authentic signals of pain from sitting too long on a threadbare cushion and to squash the fires of sexual desire by blanket celibacy, even though that might not be good for our relationships or our health. While overidentifying with our physical form reifies the sense of separation and ultimately limits our freedom, at the same time, our human vessel is a profound mystical system. If you are called to live in the world and serve its evolution, it is important to approach your body and the forces that move it with reverence.

Most people I know have a complicated relationship with their body. For some, it is a source of shame when the body refuses to yield to their will to be slimmer, fitter, or wrinkle- and cellulite-free. For others, it is a source of pride that swallows their attention in endless cosmetic maintenance to ensure desirability. Sometimes when challenged with sickness, the body can feel like a prison of pain. Perhaps you feel awkward in your body, trying to ignore its embarrassing quirks and cravings. Even when you finally learn to accept your form, being a human animal brings a mixture of gifts and challenges.

WHAT *IS* A HUMAN BODY?

All wisdom teachings invite us to know that our subtle depths are not limited to the contours, age, or shape of our form. Disidentifying with the body as who we are makes sense given that the body is destined to be temporary. Yet this vehicle is way more than it seems. All bodies contain subtle energetic portals that have the potential to transmit great love and beauty, bridging the gap between heavenly and earthly realms of being. Taoists, rishis, and Kabbalists all discovered maps to track our subtle energetic physiology, each developing healing philosophies and practices that help the body to open and become more refined so there can be more traffic between the realms. Given that the body is the densest aspect of our consciousness and the slowest to change, practices like hatha yoga and qigong and somatic modalities like cranial osteopathy and acupuncture can be very helpful in awakening and vivifying the body so it can integrate refined spiritual states.

Even when you know you are not your body, there is no escaping the forces of life that move through us all. Common to all animals, human beings have three primary instincts: the drive to survive, the drive for pleasure, and the drive to belong. These drives are more powerful than a nuclear bomb, forming the underbelly of our humanity. They directly influence everything we do but often remain in the unconscious. To paraphrase Carl Jung, that which remains in the unconscious appears in our lives as fate. Deny or try to push past these forces, and they inevitably end up sabotaging our cherished spiritual intentions.

I am sure you have heard incidents of seemingly realized masters falling from Grace into some painful acting out. Inevitably, spiritual abuse always has something to do with these instinctual drives spilling out sideways, manifesting as primitive behavior with sex, money, or power. Sadly, it brings immense devastation and often undermines our faith in the lofty teachings and transmission they shared. The more light that flows through our vessel, the more pressure it will put on anything that is not fully integrated. Whatever our state of spiritual realization, as long as we still have a body, it is not wise to think we are over being a human animal.

Living the embodiment of Grace requires a different approach than merely trying to subjugate, repress, or transcend these drives, as has been the classical spiritual approach for Christian mystics, Hindu ascetics, and Buddhist monks and nuns. Those approaches might work well within a monastic setting, but I have not seen them work well for those living in the West. As long as the body is here, these drives are here. It serves us better to understand and befriend them. Then perhaps like a well-treated pet, they can curl up in our lap and relax, ceasing to cause trouble. Perhaps they could even help us to live a full-bodied, integrated, juicy realization.

UNEARTHING OUR GUILTY SECRETS

I cannot count the number of times a mature practitioner finally plucked up the courage to confess something they felt deeply ashamed of still being caught in. I can almost predict what they are about to tell me: a pattern of compulsive overeating they just cannot seem to stop or some illicit sexual compulsion, either with pornography or an affair they know is not healthy and could deeply hurt another. Often, it is an addictive need to maintain their social status at the top of some pecking order, even though it contradicts their egalitarian values. I always feel great compassion when hearing these kinds of "confessions." I know how powerful these forces can be, even when we understand that letting them run our life is destructive to our spiritual integrity.

Since our instinctual drives are the primal hungers of the human animal, they have a "guttural" feel. They rarely flow through filters of reason. Rather, they are about immediate gratification. That can lead us to act from instinct only, without thinking of the consequences. How can we be graceful with this? It starts with refusing to hide in shame about being a human animal. This means accepting that it is normal to have wants, needs, and desires. If you insist that you should not have them, then there will be no option but for the instinctual part of your nature to go underground into the shadow. This guarantees that at some point, when you least expect it, your animal nature will seep out of you sideways, causing trouble. It is much wiser to understand and integrate these drives.

THE SELF-PRESERVATION DRIVE

Let us begin by bowing to the brilliance of our self-preservation instinct, without which none of us would be here. This drive sparks the signals in your mind and body that say, "Time to eat." If you listen, it will also tell you what to eat and when to stop, to rest when you're tired (rather than drink more coffee), and to move when you feel stagnant. This force naturally drives you to take shelter in a storm, get out of the way of oncoming traffic, remove yourself from an unsafe environment, save for retirement, and make smart choices that provide basic security and comfort.

Our self-preservation instinct is all about keeping the body and mind alive, thriving, regulated, and stable. When this instinct is balanced, you naturally do what is needed to create a workable foundation for your practical well-being. A balanced self-preservation instinct helps you be more grounded and graceful in ordinary life. It serves your deepening realization by not creating unnecessary survival stress (thus supporting a life of ego relaxation).

Dismiss this instinct, and you will likely struggle with self-care. When you ignore, push past, or dismiss the intelligence of the survival instinct, you might resist going to sleep at a reasonable hour, forget to eat regularly, or struggle to find a regular rhythm of shopping for and cooking healthy food. This sets you up for weight or health problems.

The self-preservation instinct also governs your relationship to money and security. Dismissing this instinct might express as not tracking your spending or neglecting to find a sustainable source of income. You might be following your bliss but not paying attention to the practical viability of it.

A further level of devolution is being caught in the grip of one of your instincts. Gripped by your self-preservation drive, you become either very disassociated from your body or overly obsessed with it. Both extremes elicit guttural, primitive behavior that inhibits graceful embodiment. For example, gripped by your self-preservation drive, you can get greedy, always chasing after more money, even at the expense of your relationships, inner peace, or stress levels. You might spend impulsively, without being aware of how much debt you are racking up. You can become obsessed with your exercise regimen or body-fat percentage and then swing the other way, binging without brakes like a pig at a hog trough. You can become overly attached to your creature comforts, turning having the "right" foods into a neurotic attachment that takes away from the simplicity of eating what the body needs, in moderate amounts, with flexibility in different situations. You can turn anything that originally was designed to help you settle and regulate into a false idol. Whenever you bow down to a false god, you suffer.

THE SEXUAL DRIVE

Sexuality is a huge subject that warrants several books. Our focus here is how the sexual drive affects our capacity to embody Grace. Reflect for a moment on how you and I came to be here. Clearly our very existence was ignited into being by a powerful, juicy desire to connect in ecstatic pleasure with another. What is this force that caused your parents to find one another so interesting? What causes the dance of masculine and feminine? What causes the force of creation to meet and merge with itself? When we look freshly at this juicy, sweet, vibrant force that runs through our bodies, as well as the plant and animal kingdoms, how could we not bow to the mystery?

The sexual drive makes life delicious and pleasurable. In its purity, the sexual instinct can surely take us to God, opening us through ecstasy to let ananda flow through our nerves. Powerfully rejuvenating, it turns us on, not just to mate but also to grow, connect, share, and discover creative new possibilities. Obviously when our bodies are younger, Mother Nature wants us to do our part in propagating the species. Yet aging and fluctuating hormones do not have to be the end, for Eros is not merely genital. There are many ways this pleasurable ignition of life can flow, whether you have a partner to enjoy it with or not—for example, by letting your body surrender to the beat of some fabulous music, getting high on the scent of roses freshly picked from your garden, or appreciating the sensual pleasure of slicing an avocado, sprinkling it with salt and fresh lime, and savoring how it melts in your mouth. You can relish the decorating of your new home, playing with paint colors in different lights and textured fabrics that soothe and stimulate the senses. Even getting dressed in the morning can be an embodiment of sensual enrichment that makes you so glad to be alive. When your sexual drive is in balance, you feel the sheer pleasure of existence. You have zip and energy and enthusiasm. You naturally want to create some kind of beauty—be it in the home, in your work, or in the world. Your way of being becomes richer, juicier, more artful.

When this drive is dismissed, suppressed, or ignored, you feel stagnant, unfulfilled, and dry. The life-giving force that lives in your sexual organs is literally the energetic pump that circulates nourishing energy to smooth out the rough edges. When this is stagnant, you tend to be harder, edgier, and not much fun to be around. It often plays a part in depression. At the very least, your human body needs to be touched, and not necessarily with sexual intent. Simply put, skin-on-skin contact with other human animals is a primary need. Even basic touch, like the warmth of a hand reaching for our own or a kind hug from a friend, triggers the release of stress-relieving hormones such as oxytocin that help our whole being relax and open up.

Many years ago, I had a shy, single, gay client come to me for regular spiritual counseling sessions. Without thinking about it, I would naturally put my hand on the back of his heart, just giving it a little rub as he walked out the door. It was a nonverbal embodiment of my care for him. Many months into our work together, he told me that he so looked forward to that simple touch. It was so powerful he would sit in his car and cry with relief, driving home much lighter. That magical, healing exchange of energy with others can often do more for us than anything else.

Yet it is very easy to get gripped by our sexual drive into ungraceful ways of being. When we overidentify with our body, not only are we objectifying ourselves but we cannot help but objectify others, relating as if they exist to meet our needs. This can make us energetically greedy, pulling for satiation, affirmation, or manipulation with our sexual magnetism. This erodes the true life-enhancing beauty of Eros into an egoic exchange, ultimately leaving us unsatisfied. We are equally gripped by the sexual drive when we just close the door to touch and juicy connection out of fear of getting hurt, fear of losing control, or fear of being opened to a level of vulnerability that scares us.

Given that our sexual instinct governs the pleasure and reward signals of our brain, its most difficult grip is surely the hell realm of addiction. This force naturally drives us away from pain and toward pleasure. I have observed many who have struggled with serious addiction, be it to alcohol, drugs, food, or pornography, and at the core is the drive to change our state by chasing the quick high. Driving this is inevitably some unmet anxiety, insecurity, or suffering that we have not yet been able to stay present with and feel all the way. If you have even a minor form of addiction, I strongly recommend that you be thorough with all of the earlier teachings and practices of this book and seek specialist support.

THE SOCIAL DRIVE

We will come home together, or not at all. This succinctly captures the essence of our drive for community, to be part of a greater whole, and to somehow find our place within the greater scheme of things. Just as most animals will not survive if they find themselves outside of the herd, you will not thrive on any level in isolation. We humans are relational beings. Thus living the embodiment of Grace asks us to grow in relationship—not just in our intimate relationships but our relationships with groups of people. At the deepest level, the social drive helps to ensure not only that we do not get left out in the cold but also that our life has meaning and value as part of a greater whole.

The social drive can bring out your best to give, receive, collaborate, and share. This will ask you to evolve beyond self-centeredness, learn to speak your truth without attack, allow and appreciate differences, harmonize your talents with those of others, receive help with things you are not naturally great at, and open to the way that best serves the whole. We all want this, but if you have spent a week living under the same roof as your family of origin, you surely know that it is easier being an angel when no one is ruffling your feathers.

Maintaining real connection with groups of people can be a challenge. I have taught within pioneering intentional communities, all who have gathered around agreed spiritual principles, such as Venwoude in the Netherlands, the Findhorn Foundation in Scotland, and the Esalen Institute in California. Furthermore, I have founded two spiritual communities, in the United Kingdom and the United States. Even when everyone sincerely gives their best, it is not always easy to let go of "my" way and harmonize around "the" way. Being graceful with the social instinct does not mean withholding how you really feel to keep the semblance of harmony. It asks you to participate authentically with your "tribe"—be that your family tribe, your local community, your fellow spiritual companions, your colleagues, or your cluster of friends. This is ultimately an ongoing inquiry throughout our life.

If you dismiss the importance of the social drive, you will likely end up isolating yourself from circles of support. You then run the risk of becoming off center in many ways, purely because of the lack of objective feedback that can only come from the reflections of many. You can get subsumed in your work and become overly eccentric, unbalanced, or just plain disconnected. When your life lacks the stimulation of varied kinds of conversation, you become too narrow. Even if you are an exceptionally gifted artist, musician, writer, or coach, ultimately your art form does not fully flourish without cross-fertilization with others. Some of the most fertile moments in the evolution of philosophy, art, science, and spirituality emerged when individuals with different kinds of illumination came together, as in the Renaissance or around the ancient Great Library of Alexandria.

When gripped by the social instinct, we become obsessed with keeping up appearances and being successful in the world. We instinctually orient ourselves toward what preserves our status as an important person in the pecking order of our choice. This can suck us into being obsessed with outer symbols of success, such as the latest car, stylish clothes, or a trophy partner. It most commonly takes the form of staying connected to those we believe are the important people, often relegating others to the B-list. This is all an unconscious attempt to get value, meaning, and affirmation from others. Author Neal Rogin calls it "opinion management." It can swallow our life force into endless rounds of hot air through some of the lowest forms of social media. Bow to this false idol, and it will devour meaningful relating and block the flow of Grace in your life.

The following inquiry and meditation practices are designed to help you see where you can significantly tune the dial on your ongoing spiritual practice and show you exactly where you most need to practice presence.

INQUIRY **Integrating Your Instinctual Forces**

Perhaps, dear reader, just by reading this chapter you are gaining insights on what parts of your animal humanity you tend to dismiss and how that diminishes the embodiment of Grace in your life. You might have seen where you are most vulnerable to getting gripped. Whatever is emerging, it is crucial that you view this with compassion for your humanity. Remember, there is no one alive that does not have to ride these forces of life.

Which instinctual force most bumps you out of spiritual integrity?
If you are not sure, explore where you have the most trouble in your ordinary life, where you find yourself acting contrary to your deepest prayers. Refuse to demonize yourself for this.

Allowing space for this force to be here, what's the energy within it?
What is this actually like in your body? For example, do you feel it most in your deep belly, pelvis, genitals, mouth, or hands? Remember, the instinctual forces are primary hungers, so let yourself feel this hunger for what it is.

Opening into the energy within this instinctual force, what is the true need here?
See if you can welcome that true animal human need, just as you have been learning to allow everything else.

Feel into the deepest prayer for your life. Your purest motivation for being. Now ask: *What's truly needed for my animal drives to harmonize with the prayer of my deepest heart?*

Journal what comes to you, and commit to one action that embodies this wisdom. ~

MEDITATION **Circulating the Nectars**

This meditation is inspired by a practice that I learned many years ago from Taoist master Mantak Chia. It also synthesizes elements from the Mountain of Presence practice (chapter 3) and Resting in the Shower of Grace (chapter 7). It is powerfully rejuvenating and nourishing and is a great support for integrating the body of teachings and practices we have worked with in this journey. This is a great practice to do if you find yourself gripped by any instinct. It is also great to do if you have been feeling a little dull energetically.

1. Sit in your sacred space where you will not be disturbed.

2. Focus on the rise and fall of your breath. Let each inhale call you deeper into the present moment, into your body, into presence. Let each exhale invite melting.

3. Receiving the holding of the cushion, chair, or floor, take in the ground underneath you. Not just the physical ground of the earth you can see and sense but that primordial ground of Grace, with its power and dynamism. Feel as if you are sitting in that mountain of

presence, in and part of the primordial foundation. Stay there until you feel deep, grounded, and settled.

4. Simultaneously, receive that shower of light that contains every blessing, all love, as if the molecules of light themselves carry the Grace of all the enlightened beings, bodhisattvas, and subtle forces of Grace. Just as the light of the sun that creates the day is already here, feel this sense of being in that shower of light, love, and refined qualities.

5. Now feel this ground of Grace and shower of light starting to circulate throughout your body. Beginning with the base of your spine, very softly "pulse" the perineum as you breathe in, and feel the energy and dynamism of the ground of Grace move up the back body. At the top of the breath, feel the energy moving up and over the crown of the head. On the exhale feel the shower of Grace and all subtle nectars pour down the front body, bringing all the nourishment you could possibly need.

6. As the breath cycle completes, pulse the perineum very gently on the in breath, feeling the life-force energy moving up the back body, reaching over the crown, and then on the exhale feel that divine shower pouring nectar through your front body again.

7. Find your rhythm with the breath, sensing and visualizing, letting the forces of life itself move through your body and subtle body, including and harmonizing all dimensions of your being—from the most primal to the most subtle. You might find that you feel your feet beginning to "drink" from the energy of the earth as well. You might feel as if your entire body is drinking subtle nectars that circulate more smoothly and freely as your practice progresses. This tends to happen when the practice gets more established.

A further development of this practice is letting it become part of a walking meditation in nature, taking in the ground of Grace through your feet and lower body and receiving the shower of Grace as you receive the sunlight. Feel these forces of life itself revitalizing, renewing, and rebalancing body, heart, and mind. ~

The more you befriend rather than try to transcend your animal humanity with its needs, wants, and drives, the more it ceases to be an obstacle. Rather, you recognize its value as a holy vehicle for experience and cocreative expression. Honoring the sacredness of all forms while remembering the mystery that is always animating them, you naturally become more graceful here in the hubris of it all. You grow more balanced, moderate, and kind in the way you respond to the true needs of the body, listening to the invitations that aging, menopause, and even sickness bring. Perhaps more than anything else, this embrace grows you into your fullest humanity.

16 BEING THE PRESENCE OF LOVE

There is a way of breathing that's a shame and a suffocation,
and there's another way of expiring,
a love breath,
that lets you open infinitely.

RUMI, *The Illuminated Rumi* (translated by Coleman Barks)

The deeper your practice of ego relaxation, the more you feel the living presence coming alive inside of you. Like a fountain that circulates its nectar, yet spills over to hydrate the surrounding ground, the qualities of your true nature naturally want to be embodied and extended. Quite literally, your body, mind, heart, hands, voice, relationships, all of your life's experiences, and even your instinctual drives exist ultimately to transmit Grace. How can your human vessel be put to the best possible use down here on Earth?

The answer, as you already know, has something to do with love.

We all want love and need love at every stage of life. Yet in our culture, we bandy the word *love* about, Hallmark style, but in a way that often lacks gravity. We might say, "Love ya!" with a casual wave goodbye, or "I love you," when what we really mean is, "Can you please give me some reassurance that you love me too?" This is better than holding our heart back, but love's presence is so much deeper than a transaction to make us feel secure. It is deeper than a positive emotion. Love is who we are minus any defenses. It is our heart at rest as pure Being.

Before you can be the presence of love, you first have to receive it. Inevitably, this means relaxing your search for love. Cease demanding that it come through your preferred channels. (If you would like more help with this, please explore my audio book, *Meditations on Boundless Love*.) Only when you relax your demands for love can you begin to feel love's presence already here with every breath, in every sound, in all that your eyes light upon. The more you live into the themes and practices in this book, the more you recognize that love is always here, even when you have just received a cancer diagnosis.

A DIVINE TRANSMISSION

Love's presence is not something that can be explained or taught. I can only share how I know it and invite you to reflect on your experience. When I sit with someone who sincerely wishes to surrender, love is a divine transmission that pours out like an ocean of nourishing golden nectar. Its presence pervades my body, exuding a warm, healing glow of unconditional allowing. Eyes of the heart perceive the precious beauty of the living, breathing mystery sitting before me. Love's presence even changes my vision. Hard edges of form disappear, stripping everything back to its pure essence. I am completely transparent in the timeless now, just being no-thing and no-one, yet utterly fulfilled.

If words are needed, they come without effort. If some gesture or action is needed, that happens. Things flow, with a richness and meaning. Being love's presence is natural when sitting with a student, at the bedside of a sick husband, or when a friend has received some devastating news. In these moments love is all that matters. However, it can be so easy to forget amidst the busyness of an ordinary day. Living love's presence is ongoing moment-to-moment practice.

A few days before Christmas, I was driving my usual route to Whole Foods. While I waited at the stoplight, I noticed a homeless woman. There is often a homeless person at this traffic light, but that day, I took a closer look, taking her more fully in. I read her sign, explaining that she has lost her job, her home, and is living in her car. I feel sorry that her life is so tough, that so many people's lives are so tough. As I reach into my wallet and pull out $20, I hear the voices of others inside saying, "She will probably just drink this away," "Don't be a fool—better to give to a formal charity," or even "This is just your white middle-class guilt." I ignore their advice.

It is cold, and while I will never know whether this moment of generosity translated into a hot meal or a bottle of whiskey that night, what I do know is that as I opened the window of my car to give her that cash, our eyes met in an exchange that had nothing to do with money. It was the spontaneous embodiment of a prayer: "May the tides turn in a kinder direction for this woman and for us all. Amen." Pervading this interaction was the transmission of love's presence. It saw fit to deliver an important message within those twenty seconds before the light turned green: we all matter, we all have value, every single one of us is loved, and to hang in there even when things look like such a hopeless mess. So what if that message has to be delivered by a stranger at the stoplight?

Reflect on your experience, and perhaps you'll see that life unfurls in cycles, sometimes joyful, sometimes very painful, and in proportions that often do not feel fair. We will all have to bear things that feel unbearable, whether from sickness, old age, bereavement, or watching a family member wrestle with the demon of addiction. Strangely, it is often in these extreme moments that we become receptive for pure realms beyond our making or understanding to pour through. Heaven comes to earth if we are willing to drop out of the commentating mind and just be here, keeping our heart as open as possible, flowing with what is most natural.

GRACE BRINGS WHAT IS NEEDED

Every one of us is capable of being a Grace-delivery device, in and amidst the ordinary moments of a regular day. It does not matter whether you have a degree, how old you are, or what you think you know spiritually. One of the most powerful transmissions of Grace I have ever seen poured through the tiny frail body of a ninety-year-old great-grandmother. Her time-worn hands moved to tenderly cup the face of another in an impossible moment of loss. The living presence radiated pure, simple, perfectly attuned words, but the Grace poured not just from her mouth. Like a powerful beam of light penetrating through her entire vessel, it poured directly into the marrow of another, saying, "You are not alone. Love is here. You will get through this."

It is stunning how the mystery of Grace always brings forth precisely what is needed. Often this is different than what you think you need or what you think another needs. If you stay present as love, without an agenda, the specifics come forward naturally. Love's presence does not even need words. Often, love is most eloquent in the silence we share, through a kind gaze, a warm smile, or a humanizing goodness that lets another go first in the traffic. Ego relaxation gets your mind out of the way so the fountain can flow deeper into this world.

MAKE PRESENCE YOUR PRIORITY

Being the presence of love hinges on your capacity to be more fully present. That means the commentating mind is dropped into the cave of the heart, grounded in the immediacy of the body, here and now. Staying intimate with your direct experience, relishing the rise and fall of each breath, and feeling the sensation of your feet on the ground helps you live ego relaxation while making your children's lunch, speaking to a colleague on Skype, or driving to your various errands.

Even when you are dedicated to embodying Grace, it is easy to become preoccupied with your concerns and creative projects. A subtle narcissism can creep in, making you oblivious to the invitations within the seemingly minor interactions of any day. Perhaps the greatest challenge to being the presence of love in our present culture is bowing down to the false god of technology. Automatically obeying the demanding ping of every text, email, and Facebook notification will scatter your energy in multiple directions. This is a disaster if you sincerely wish to embody a more graceful way of being, as it will keep you living on the surface of yourself.

Although our present culture worships speed over elegance of action, neuroscience has verified what we intuitively know, that multitasking is significantly disintegrative to the brain. Your budding realization, not to mention your health, social, and relational well-being, requires that you have some uninterrupted time to just be. Furthermore, your presence cannot deepen without cultivating one-pointed concentration. I highly recommend turning all unnecessary notifications on your electronic devices off. Besides, who really wants to receive a Facebook post reporting on what you ate for dinner? Let us use technology wisely in ways that support the embodiment of Grace rather than hamper it.

LOVE AMIDST THE GRIT

Being the presence of love is not all sweetness and light. Inevitably in our loving of one another, we arrive at junctures that can be very challenging to navigate gracefully. What does it mean to be the presence of love in the face of relational friction?

Love itself does not force, yet it *is* the most powerful force. It wants to melt your armor, melt anything about you that is fixed, frozen, or fake so it can unfold deeper into this world. Often we do not even know cobwebs of closure exist in us until someone we live with shines a light on them. If you have been in a committed relationship, you know how challenging it can be when you trip over that same old argument you have been having with your beloved since the start. One night, when my husband and I were bumping up against a stubborn wall, I prayed a very practical, honest prayer: "*Help*! And help us be receptive to the help!"

The details of how our prayers are answered, heard, or even matter is a bigger conversation for another book. But later that night, after giving it up to Grace and hanging out in that mystery of unknowing, I began to feel the loving presence coming online inside, as if a blocked fountain was starting to gurgle again. A game-changing insight arrived: "Love always includes and integrates only what is true in all diverging perspectives."

I recognized that this is the evolutionary pulse at work in nature. She gracefully allows death of forms that are no longer useful but at the same time does not reject or waste anything. Everything is integrated into a higher expression that is more useful in the now. The winter ice pack melts to become waterfalls. Plants harmonize around one another, adapting to survive specific climates. I was asked to make space for the truth in my husband's perspective but not the ego defense in it, and to include the truth in my perspective but not the ego defense in it. We are never asked to surrender to any ego distortion, only to a deeper truth. I have found this resolves any battle of wills because it evolves us beyond the attachments, positions, and identifications of "I" and "my." This is how love triumphs, and everyone wins. Thank you. Amen.

Embracing the grit within our human relating is how love's presence continues to evolve us. It always provides an opportunity to learn something, to let go of something, to allow space for more love to extend itself. This awakens you to the fact that your relationships with others, even with their imperfections, are such gifts. If you knew you were seeing your dear friend or beloved spouse for the very last time in this world, wouldn't the most real thing you could possibly say be, "Thank you for everything. It's been a privilege. I love you."

TRUE EXPRESSION OF LOVE

Authentic awakening always results in feeling more love toward all beings. The more your sense of separation dissolves, the more a spontaneous kindness pours forth, and that makes you less self-centered and naturally more generous, not just with a few special people but with everyone. While your mind feels deliciously empty of that crackling old radio station of the past, your heart takes on a fullness, expressing many of the most important qualities of humanity: compassion, empathy, joy, strength, courage. You start to feel the palpable presence of love as your deepest heart.

Given that our world is often so lacking in real love, you will likely feel the nudge to not hold back from expressing it. Aldous Huxley, in his final summation, said, "It is a bit embarrassing to have been concerned with the human problem all one's life and find at the end that one has no more to offer by way of advice than 'Try to be a little kinder.'"[1] While you are at it, see if you can be a little more appreciative.

Acknowledge your brother or sister for the tireless work they are doing on behalf of your aging parents. Say a sincere thank you to your husband, your mother, or your friend for bearing with you through the latest trial or simply for cooking a delicious dinner. Be a little more patient with your children as you encourage them to do their homework. Be a little more forgiving with yourself when you stumble in ignorance, again.

When love's presence is moving freely, that hollow sense of deprivation is no more. You become naturally generous because you are abiding within and part of the abundant source. Just as the water moves through the central axis of the fountain's vessel and evenly extends outward before it loops back up again, love's presence circulates through your body, heart, and mind and dissolves self-centered concerns. It also dissolves the sense of who is "giver" and who is "receiver," eradicating any sense of sacrifice. Rather, you feel the flow of Grace, circulating through your human vessel.

MAGNETIZING THE MIRACULOUS

One of the questions I am asked most often, usually toward the end of a retreat when everyone is feeling their inner cup running over, is how they can help someone who seems desperately stuck or sick. I am sure there is someone in your immediate circle of family, friends, or loved ones who is in a bad way, whether through addiction, deep depression, an eating disorder, or worse. These pernicious forms of suffering always require specialist treatment. Yet is there anything spiritually that you, as a family member or caring friend, can do to help? Yes, there is.

Being the presence of love can take the form of holding the vision of another's highest nature and refusing to see them only as their problem. This is a much better use of your energy than worrying about them or judging them for walking down a dark path. You might recall that trust is really the placement of your psychic attention. Right now, try this experiment. Consider the person whom you wish you could help (you could also do this for a country or a specific group of people). First, notice how it feels in your body, heart, and mind to place your trust in the forces of their ego. Now, notice how it feels in your body, heart, and mind to place your trust in the forces of their true nature to emerge through this and thrive.

I am sure you notice an immediate difference. One leads you to feel hopeless and worried and might result in you withdrawing from being present as love with that person. The latter will make you into a powerfully healing presence in their life, even if there is nothing specific that you do or say. Your trust in their capacity will transmit in some way as love. Imagine how it would feel if the roles were reversed. Would it feel more helpful to be around someone regarding you as your problem or someone who is holding the vision that you are more than this, that you will find your way and might even come to thrive?

When you place your trust not in another's ego, but in their higher nature, you are spiritually calling it forward. With that woman at the stoplight, love's unspoken transmission was also communicating, "It does not have to be this way." Sometimes we need another to hold a possibility for us that we struggle to claim for ourselves. At this joining, not at the level of personality, but essence to essence, the door for the miraculous can open. I have witnessed so many extraordinary leaps in consciousness that it has taught me never to give up on anyone—to always hold the possibility for another's transformation, even when it looks hopeless. Through Grace, it never is.

LOVING PRESENCE IN BODY, HEART, AND MIND

In time, with sincere devotion to your practice of ego relaxation, all four dimensions of Grace begin to synthesize. You feel a fuller, freer flow moving through your three primary centers: body, heart, and mind.

Your body takes on a grounded immediacy. You feel more substantial, as if truly inhabiting this vehicle in the present, even though you likely feel way "bigger" than your physical form. Presence itself always has that sense of fullness, of is-ness, making your actions more direct, clean, and potent. Just as a plant is nourished by its roots in the soil of the Earth and its leaves reaching toward the activating light of the sun, you feel what Vedic philosophy calls prana flowing through your body. You feel alive, more open, and energized. You might have felt a hint of this in the meditation in the previous chapter.

Love's presence is by definition heart-full. The more you discover that nothing bad will happen if you stay present and feel everything, the more your heart can open. Compassion, empathy, joy, kindness, and courage can flow. When a hurt closes the door of your heart, compassion and forgiveness help it heal. In the process, it calls you into a whole other depth of heart where everything is resolved and absolved. On first glance this might look rather wet, sentimental. Interestingly, love's presence also purifies the heart of attachment to your story. Thus, the fountain flows through the heart with objectivity, supporting not just personal expressions of love but universal love.

Love's presence has a deeply settling effect on our entire being, and this includes the mind. Often the mind will not calm because you likely have been living too long in a state of agitation. Love's presence first soothes and then settles a jumpy mind so you drop out of the patterned ego mind that is always referencing the past. Then, love's presence is powerfully peaceful. It might feel as if your head is a vast open window to the sky, pervaded by a loving light and shimmering awareness. You see and know, yet not through historically based filters. This refines and expands your perception, giving way to unified vision.

Perhaps it makes more sense to you now why the instructions for every inquiry practice in this book have encouraged you to let the questions into your somatic experience, your felt experience, as well as your awareness. Including all three centers of your vessel as you practice supports a balanced, integrated awakening. You might even start to feel as if your deep belly, your heart, and your head are three specific spouts of the fountain that begin to overflow in synchronicity, circulating the nectar of love's presence exponentially.

The following inquiry supports you to move through your day as a living fountain.

INQUIRY **Being the Presence of Love**

At first, I recommend sharing this inquiry question with a friend or else meditating into it as you have already been doing. Then, write the two questions on a sticky note and place it on your computer, the dashboard of your car, your fridge, or wherever you like. May it remind you to continuously yield to the living presence that knows exactly how to be love in and amidst the flow of your everyday life.

What's it like, in body, heart, and mind when presence is your priority? Get detailed and familiar with how it feels, in all three of your centers, when you are truly at home inside. Stay with this for at least ten minutes.

What does it mean, right now, to "be" love?
Being the presence of love is dynamic and ever unfolding, ever fresh, and precisely attuned to each situation. Perhaps it means being present and engaging with the checkout clerk at your supermarket, enjoying the exchange. Sometimes being love means listening more substantially, not just to words but to the unspoken. If you stay close to these questions, a most potent, beautiful, complete embodiment will find its way through you, moment to moment. ~

If you are sufficiently present, you recognize there is a deep sweetness to life itself. Ramana Maharshi beautifully said, "When your real, effortless, joyful nature is realized, it will not be inconsistent with the ordinary activities of life."[2] The simple moments where love is being radiated and circulated have the most meaning. At the end of life and at the beginning of life, when the veils between the realms are thinnest, we often see clearly what existence is really all for—*love*. You are an embodiment of the deepest Grace. Love is its signature.

EPILOGUE

Yes . . . and Thank You

I do not claim to know the mystery of Grace:
only that it meets us where we are,
and does not leave us where it found us.

ANNE LAMOTT, ***Traveling Mercies: Some Thoughts on Faith***

In the end, the way of Grace asks you to just keep surrendering, which means saying yes to the invitations that come knocking mysteriously on your door. Just as a plant is sometimes pruned back in order for robust new growth to emerge, can you say yes when it is time to let go of something no longer useful? Welcome the pruning of subtle judgment, pride, commentary, or anything that blocks your capacity to stay present, openhearted, and awake. Remember that you do not do the pruning. Ego relaxation shows you how to say yes when it is asked. Everything exposed to the light will itself become light.

Keep saying yes to that which fertilizes your soul. Cherish the practices you have found to help you to stay intimate with your deepest heart and to be quiet and settled in your boundless nature so you can listen and respond elegantly as the embodiment of Grace amidst your daily life. If you make the teachings and practices in this book your cherished friends, perhaps integrating your favorites into your daily rhythm, Grace can become exponential within you and extend its nectars more substantially into our world. For everyone's sake, say yes to that.

Keep saying yes to the mystery of how everything is always happening all at once—the beauty and the horror—but somehow there is

Grace to help us get through it, whether in the guise of friends, nature, these teachings, or subtle blessings from celestial spheres. Every time you say yes, anything untrue in you is dissolved. Grace will always deepen, season, and bring out the very best in you.

Whenever you feel the living presence coming alive within your direct experience, you cannot help but say "thank you." The arrival of gratitude within your heart is recognition that Grace is, and you are bowing in recognition. You naturally say "thank you" when you have a close brush with danger and make it through relatively unscathed, when love somehow triumphs even amidst the spectacular imperfection of your family dynamic, or when someone central to your life has been given a clean bill of health. You say "thank you" not to something else. Perhaps you still do not know to whom you are saying "thank you," but you say it anyway because you know that it is the truth. Something precious is revealed as you are lifted out of stress and struggle: You are part of this Grace. You are its embodiment, always and forever. As you keep returning the divine gaze, you become its reflection.

> Now that you have learned to be as melting snow,
> Grace is your unchanging ground.
>
> Now that you have learned to recognize and receive
> the subtle blessings, Grace is your sustenance.
>
> Now that you have learned to yield even into the
> fierce forces, Grace is your transformer.
>
> Now, together, let us live as the fountain we were
> made to be. Let the living waters flow to quench
> our parched and tired Earth.

ACKNOWLEDGMENTS

Thank you to my beloved husband, Bob Duchmann, for all your love, support, and understanding during the writing process and for your equal dedication to spiritual service. Thank you to my students at the Sonoma and Marin sangha, my online students, private counseling clients, and all who have attended retreats since 2007. It is your questions, grapplings, and sincerity that have drawn these teachings forward into the world. Thank you to my former students at the OneSpirit Interfaith Foundation for growing me as a teacher. Thank you to my editor, Gretel Hakanson, for your unswerving dedication to this book and superb guidance at every stage. Thank you to everyone at Sounds True, whom I am honored to collaborate with. Thank you to Russ Hudson, for writing such a generous foreword and for being such a light in this world. Thank you to Mirabai Starr for giving this reluctant, dyslexic spiritual teacher the nudge to write. Thank you to Parthenia Hicks, Kelly Notaras, and Barbara Moulton for support with the initial proposal. Thank you to everyone who read segments or helped with research: Richard Redmond, Neal Rogin, David Nichol, Gabrielle Beard, Cass Cartlett, and Yosi Amram. Thank you to my friends Lama Palden, Stephen Dinan, Devaa Harley Mitchell, Jacqueline Chan, Shauna Shapiro, Tara Herron, Diane Berke, Kellie O'Boyle, Katherine Armer, and Roger Housden, and thank you to Caroline Muir for being my American angel.

Thank you to my family in Australia and also to my family in California.

Thank you to everyone at the Shift Network, especially Carol Anne Robinson. Thank you to the mentors who support this work in the online programs: Brianna Delott, Kathy Stewart, Jolijn Olthuis, Mary Campbell. Thank you to all who have supported this work in the United Kingdom and Europe: Jenny Grainger, Heather Pozzo, Martin Nathanael, Camilla Bergman, Bella Cranmore, Ade Adjenji, Anja Saunders, and the Venwoude community. Thank you to my team: Shellie Beck, for your tireless work and devotion behind the scenes, and Jon Leland and Brooks Cole.

I owe so much to all of my teachers: Thank you to John Leebold, Jim Leonard, Annette Stein, the late Rabbi Joseph Gelberman, and Tom and Linda Carpenter, for nurturing me in the early years. Deep gratitude for the transmission I received from Mother Meera. I am deeply grateful to A. H. Almaas and Karen Johnson for their infinite generosity, luminous wisdom, and service to so many. An especially deep bow for Jeanne Hay—your tireless love and dedication support me to continue integrating, refining, and discovering.

Thank you is insufficient for the unspeakable blessings and inner instruction received from Siva Sakthi Ammaiyar, the naked beauty of the Kashmiri feminine mystic Lalla, and the light of the Holy Spirit.

Finally, I offer deepest salutations to Sri Ramana Maharshi, whose living presence came alive in that cave and claimed me as his own. I am eternally grateful and devoted.

NOTES

Introduction

1. Rumi, *The Illuminated Rumi*, ed. Coleman Barks (New York: Broadway Books, 1997), 103.

Chapter 1. Surrender: The Practice of Ego Relaxation

1. Rumi, *The Essential Rumi*, eds. Coleman Barks and John Moyne (New York: HarperCollins, 1995), 13.
2. Rumi, *The Essential Rumi*, 70.

Chapter 2. There Is Nothing to Fear

1. Hafiz, *The Gift*, trans. Daniel Ladinsky (New York: Penguin Compass, 1999), 234.

Chapter 3. Melting the Grip of Control

1. Matthew Greenblatt, *The Essential Teachings of Ramana Maharshi: A Visual Journey* (Agoura Hills, CA: Inner Directions, 2002), 65.
2. Chögyam Trungpa, dharma talk (Boulder, CO, 1987).
3. Hafiz, *The Gift*, 127.

Chapter 4. Dropping the Knife of Judgment

1. Foundation for Inner Peace, *A Course in Miracles: Manual for Teachers* (Mill Valley, CA: Foundation for Inner Peace, 1976), 27.
2. Chögyam Trungpa, *Smile at Fear: Awakening the True Heart of Bravery*, ed. Carolyn Rose Gimian (Boston: Shambhala, 2009), 6.
3. A. H. Almaas, *Work on the Superego* (Berkeley: Diamond Books, 1992), 6.

Part II: Receiving the Blessings of Grace

1. Rumi, *The Essential Rumi*, 128.
2. Luke 12:7 (New International Version).

Chapter 5. Cultivating Trust

1. Dante Alighieri, *The Divine Comedy* (New York: New American Library, 2003), 121.

Chapter 6. Humility: Bowing to the Mystery

1. Foundation for Inner Peace, *A Course in Miracles: Workbook for Students* (Mill Valley, CA: Foundation for Inner Peace, 1980), 360.
2. Lorin Roche, *The Radiance Sutras: 112 Gateways to the Yoga of Wonder and Delight* (Boulder, CO: Sounds True, 2014), 124.

Chapter 7. Patience: The Gentle Effort

1. Loch Kelly, *Shift into Freedom: The Science and Practice of Open-Hearted Awareness* (Boulder, CO: Sounds True, 2015), 5.
2. David Godman, ed., *Be as You Are: The Teachings of Sri Ramana Maharshi* (New York: Arkana, 1985), 103.
3. Shunryu Suzuki, *Zen Mind, Beginners Mind: Informal Talks on Zen Meditation and Practice* (Boston: Shambhala, 2011), 131.
4. Gangaji, *Freedom and Resolve: Finding Your True Home in the Universe* (Ashland, OR: The Gangaji Foundation, 1999), epigraph.
5. Lama Palden Drolma in discussion with the author, November 2017.
6. Sally Kempton, *Meditation for the Love of It: Enjoying Your Own Deepest Experience* (Boulder, CO: Sounds True, 2011), 63.

Chapter 8. Entering the Joy of Being

1. World Health Organization, *Mental Health Atlas 2011*, who.int/mental_health/publications/mental_health_atlas_2011/en/.
2. Foundation for Inner Peace, *A Course in Miracles* (Mill Valley, CA: Foundation for Inner Peace, 1976), 7:11, 136.

3. Kiddushin 4:12 (Jerusalem Talmud).
4. Roche, *The Radiance Sutras*, 84.
5. Psalms 23: 5–6 (English Standard Version).

Chapter 9. Forgiveness: Transforming Heartbreak

1. Greenblatt, *Essential Teachings*, 68–9.

Chapter 10. Compassion: Loving Your Suffering

1. Pema Chödrön, *Comfortable with Uncertainty: 108 Teachings on Cultivating Fearlessness and Compassion* (Boston: Shambhala, 2002), 95.

Chapter 11. Unwinding Your Core Ego Identity

1. Roberto Assagioli, *Psychosynthesis: A Collection of Basic Writings* (New York: Viking Press, 1971), 116–17.
2. Neal Rogin, *Delightenment: Escaping the Solitary Confinement of Your Prisonality* (Novato, CA: Delightenment Press, 2017).
3. Greenblatt, *Essential Teachings*, 70.
4. Sri Nisargadatta Maharaj, *I Am That: Talks with Sri Nisargadatta Maharaj*, trans. Maurice Frydman (Durham, NC: Acorn Press, 1988), 253.
5. Foundation for Inner Peace, *A Course in Miracles*, 31:7, 622.

Chapter 12. Resting in Boundless True Nature

1. Ken Wilber, *No Boundary: Eastern and Western Approaches to Personal Growth* (Boston: Shambhala, 1979), 10.
2. John 14:2 (English Standard Version).
3. Keith Dowman, *Spaciousness: The Radical Dzogchen of the Vajra-Heart; Longchenpa's Treasury of the Dharmadhatu* (Kathmandu: Vajra Publications, 2013), 47.
4. Foundation for Inner Peace, *A Course in Miracles: Workbook for Students*, 167.
5. William Blake, "Auguries of Innocence," Poetry Foundation, accessed February 1, 2018, poetryfoundation.org/poems/43650/auguries-of-innocence.

Chapter 13. Cultivating Equanimity in Uncertain Times

1. Anandamayi Ma, *Matri Darshan: A Photo-Album about Shri Anandamayi Ma* (Stühlingen: Mangalam-Verlag Schang, 1983).

Chapter 14. Inspired Action

1. Foundation for Inner Peace, *A Course in Miracles: Manual for Teachers*, 4:1, 2.
2. Ralph Waldo Emerson, "Spiritual Laws," *Essays: First Series* (1847), accessed February 1, 2018, literaturepage.com/read/emersonessays1-80.html.
3. A. C. Bhaktivedanta Swami Pradhupāda, *The Bhagavad-Gita: As It Is* (Alachua, FL: The Bhaktivedanta Book Trust, 1983), 425.

Chapter 16. Being the Presence of Love

1. Aldous Huxley, *Moksha: Writings on Psychedelics and Visionary Experience, 1931–1963*, eds. Michael Horowitz and Cynthia Palmer (London: Chatto & Windus, 1980).
2. Greenblatt, *Essential Teachings*, 67.

ABOUT THE AUTHOR

Miranda Macpherson began her spiritual journey at the age of thirteen when, amidst a period of clinical depression, she was spontaneously opened into a profound state of boundless love. That experience initiated a lifelong dedication to spiritual practice and the study of the world's wisdom traditions. Her travels took her from her native Australia to the United Kingdom, where she founded the OneSpirit Interfaith Foundation in London, at the request of her teacher. Over the next decade, Miranda trained and ordained more than six hundred interfaith ministers and spiritual counselors, while also offering spiritual guidance to students across Europe, particularly within the Course in Miracles community.

In 2005, a seismic shift occurred that changed the course of Miranda's life. While meditating in a cave in south India that was once home to the revered sage Sri Ramana Maharshi, she experienced a direct transmission of the true nature of reality that required total surrender. In the wake of this, Miranda found herself again moving to a new continent, this time the United States. There, a body of teachings on Grace and ego relaxation began to emerge.

Today, Miranda is known for her depth of presence and gift for guiding others into direct experience of the sacred. Miranda leads the Living Grace sangha in Marin and Sonoma counties, holds retreats internationally, and offers online programs through the Shift Network. Unapologetically feminine, joyful, and down to earth in her way of being, Miranda is dedicated to loving people all the way back into the freedom and wholeness of their true nature. She lives in the San Francisco Bay Area with her husband, Bob Duchmann.

Take the *Way of Grace* teachings and practices deeper into your life with additional audio and video offerings online at mirandamacpherson.com/gracebonuses.

ABOUT SOUNDS TRUE

Sounds True is a multimedia publisher whose mission is to inspire and support personal transformation and spiritual awakening. Founded in 1985 and located in Boulder, Colorado, we work with many of the leading spiritual teachers, thinkers, healers, and visionary artists of our time. We strive with every title to preserve the essential "living wisdom" of the author or artist. It is our goal to create products that not only provide information to a reader or listener, but that also embody the quality of a wisdom transmission.

For those seeking genuine transformation, Sounds True is your trusted partner. At SoundsTrue.com you will find a wealth of free resources to support your journey, including exclusive weekly audio interviews, free downloads, interactive learning tools, and other special savings on all our titles.

To learn more, please visit SoundsTrue.com/freegifts or call us toll-free at 800.333.9185.